W9-ANN-122

The Making of Economic Reform in Eastern Europe

STUDIES OF COMMUNISM IN TRANSITION

Series Editor: Ronald J. Hill
                   Professor of Comparative Government
                   and Fellow of Trinity College,
                   Dublin, Ireland

Studies of Communism in Transition is an important series
which applies academic analysis and clarity of thought to the
recent traumatic events in Eastern and Central Europe. As
many of the preconceptions of the last half-century are cast
aside, newly independent and autonomous sovereign states are
being forced to address long-term, organic problems which had
been suppressed by, or appeased within, the communist system
of rule.

The series is edited under the sponsorship of Lorton House,
an independent charitable association which exists to advance
education in and to promote the academic study of communism and related political concepts.

The Making of Economic Reform in Eastern Europe

Conversations with Leading Reformers in Poland, Hungary and the Czech Republic

Mario I. Blejer
and
Fabrizio Coricelli

Edward Elgar

© Mario I. Blejer and Fabrizio Coricelli 1995

Published by
Edward Elgar Publishing Limited
Gower House
Croft Road
Aldershot
Hants GU11 3HR
England

Edward Elgar Publishing Company
Old Post Road
Brookfield
Vermont 05036
USA

British Library Cataloguing in Publication Data
Blejer, Mario I.
   Making of Economic Reform in Eastern Europe: Conversations
   with Leading Reformers in Poland, Hungary and the Czech
   Republic. - (Studies of Communism in Transition)
   I. Title   II. Coricelli, Fabrizio   III. Series
   338.947

Library of Congress Cataloging-in-Publication Data
Blejer, Mario I.
      The making of economic reform in Eastern Europe : conversations
   with leading reformers in Poland, Hungary, and the Czech Republic /
   Mario I. Blejer and Fabrizio Coricelli.
         p.   cm. — (Studies of communism in transition)
      Includes bibliographical references and index.
      1. Poland—Economic policy—1990- 2. Hungary—Economic
   policy—1989- 3. Czech Republic—Economic policy. 4. Statesmen—
   Europe, Eastern—Interviews. I. Coricelli, Fabrizio. II. Title. III. Series.
   HC340.3.856   1994
   338.9438—dc20   94-35019
                                                                              CIP

ISBN 1 85898 150 6

Electronic typesetting by Lorton Hall
Printed and bound in Great Britain by
Hartnolls Limited, Bodmin, Cornwall

Contents

Introduction

The political and economic reforms taking place across Eastern and Central Europe and the former Soviet bloc are among the most revolutionary developments of the late twentieth century. The analyses of the nature and causes of this tumultuous process of transformation from socialist central planning to democratic market-oriented societies have challenged virtually all established modes of studying human relations, from the purely ideological to the highly technical. In the wake of these historic and to a large extent unforeseen events, a complete new branch of economics – 'the economics of transition' – has developed, focused on explaining and providing advice concerning this unprecedented process. Although a large body of literature dealing with these issues has already appeared, no definitive analytical framework has been established, and much of what has been discussed is largely based on conjecture, most of it immediately superseded by new hypotheses or made obsolete by actual events.

This does not imply that it is not important to try to understand this process of transformation. The fact that economists are dealing with a set of unfamiliar questions does not mean that predictions and inferences cannot be made or that traditional analytical tools are not useful. However, the lack of precedents hinders analysts' ability to draw viable conclusions relevant to the current circumstances of Eastern Europe and the former Soviet Union. If it is difficult to make a proper assessment of present developments and to define a course of action with any certainty, it is even more challenging to evaluate – with any sensible historical perspective - the roles of global processes or of the myriad of individual events in the transition process itself.

The lack of a rigorous theoretical framework to design a 'scientific' transition, the absence of a historical perspective, and the unexpected nature of the revolution in Eastern Europe suggest that, although objective tendencies and developments were crucial, an extreme deterministic view, which attributes the historical events now taking place to the 'natural' course of history, remains on the surface of the phenomenon. In these circumstances, it is not difficult to overlook the fact that the process of economic reform in post-communist countries was not an autonomous inertial phenomenon, but rather was a product of human endeavour: a social, political and managerial undertaking conceived, designed and carried out by individuals. These individuals not only had to struggle without any established economic blueprints but also had to face a political environment and an expectant public that, while receptive to the idea of reforms, was apprehensive about wandering into the unknown. Even those observers not directly involved, who may find it difficult to fully grasp the scope of the dilemmas of these individuals, will have to agree that the task facing these reformers was indeed daunting.

In an attempt to understand the human dimension of the events occurring in Eastern Europe, we discussed these issues with three of the main actors in the reform process, each of whom played a key role in the design and implementation of the reform programmes in their respective countries. The three persons interviewed are: Leszek Balcerowicz, Deputy Prime Minister and Minister of Finance of Poland in 1989-91, and widely recognized as the architect of the Polish economic reforms; Peter A. Bod, currently President of the National Bank of Hungary and formerly Minister of Industry; and Václav Klaus, current Prime Minister of the Czech Republic, and at the time of the initiation of the reforms Minister of Finance of Czechoslovakia.

The interviews revolved around six interrelated themes:

(a) *Personal and intellectual formation.* This is a discussion of the intellectual, political and historical circumstances that most influenced these reformers, shaped their economic thinking, and led to their engagement in public life.

(b) *The process of thinking about the reforms.* Each reformer discusses the main factors that determined for him the objectives and concrete elements of the reform programme before its implementation.

(c) *The design of the reform package.* The relative role and importance of specific elements of the reform package are assessed and debated. The elements mentioned include currency convertibility, budgetary reforms, social safety nets, price liberalization, foreign aid, and so forth.

(d) *Expectations.* Each policy maker describes the type of expectations he had about the possible effects of the reform measures at the time that they were launched.

(e) *The actual working of the reforms and the issue of political support.* The reformers were asked to assess the success of the actual implementation of measures and to elaborate on their perspective of the political problems encountered as the reforms were being put into place. They were also asked to expand on the steps they took to muster political support for their policies and to counteract criticism and political opposition.

(f) *The prospects.* Here the reformers disclose their vision of the road ahead, forecasting in the long and short run the feasibility of a functioning market economy.

These various issues are organized in the book into four

chapters, and an appendix presents some data on each of the three countries alongside information on the basic elements of the design and performance of the reform programmes.

The dialogue with the policy makers provides comparable while sometimes very dissimilar views, reflecting both the different personalities involved and the distinct political and economic contexts. The three economists scrupulously addressed the various aspects of the reform process, presenting a candid view of their own experience and of the difficulties and satisfactions encountered in fulfilling their duties. In editing the book we decided to let the reformers speak for themselves, with a minimum of comment or rebuttal. We also decided that we should not predispose the reader by pressing our own views regarding the main lessons to be learned from the experiences or by distilling from the answers the points of agreement and disagreement. Neither do we believe that we should venture our own sentiment concerning the correctness of the reformers' judgements. We think, however, that we should stress that we emerged from these conversations with a strengthened conviction of the uniqueness of each country's experience, from its initial conditions to the specific nature of the constraints faced by the policy makers. It is indeed true that the synchronization of the regime change in various countries suggests that common, general forces were at play. Among these, the disintegration of the Soviet Union was perhaps the single most important factor, although not the only one. However, protracted economic stagnation and the attendant fear of continuously falling behind the western market economies prompted the old establishment, particularly in Hungary, to loosen the grip of central control. A similar process started, later and with more hesitation, in Poland, but it was totally absent from the political and economic scene of post-1968 Czechoslovakia. The Hungarian partial reforms, and to a certain extent the Polish ones, were carried out by the old regime in an attempt to avoid the radical break and the loss of power which in fact took place anyway. This tension between forces of change and the attempt by the old regime to survive by partially transforming itself was summarized by Timothy Garton Ash who coined, as recently as 1989, the term 'refolution', a mixture of reform and revolution.[1] As it arises from the interviews, the different degrees of 'refolution' in the three countries were an important factor constraining the type of choices made by their reformers and, before they came to power, conditioning their analytical considerations in their quest for potential and politically feasible ways of improving the functioning of their respective economies.

Reform programmes were adopted and implemented under different degrees of political pressure and in different circumstances regarding potential political unrest. Thus, for example, Poland was faced with strong and aggressive trade unions, while no such militant labour organizations were present in Czechoslovakia or Hungary. In general, as argued by Michael Bruno,[2] most reforming countries had initially a period of 'honeymoon', in which they could implement their policies in a context of generalized support by the population, but this 'honeymoon' was in fact very short. Although not surprising, it is nevertheless worthwhile to note the extent to which all three reformers carefully factored these political circumstances into their considerations, and to compare the strategies followed to address the issue.

As with many political and economic phenomena, it is

1 Timothy Garton Ash, *The Uses of Adversity* (New York: Vintage Books, 1990).
2 Michael Bruno, 'Stabilization and Reform in Eastern Europe: A Preliminary Evaluation', in M.I. Blejer, G. Calvo, F. Coricelli, and A. Gelb (eds), *Eastern Europe in Transition: From Recession to Growth?* (Washington, DC: World Bank, 1993).

tempting to associate specific reform strategies with given initial economic conditions. However, this seems to be contradicted by the actual experience of the countries considered here. For instance, the common interpretation of the Polish 'shock therapy', as the inevitable response to the hyperinflation of 1989 and to the country's huge foreign debt, fails to explain the reasons for the analogous macroeconomic programme in the former Czechoslovakia, a country characterized by a stable and balanced macroeconomic situation and no foreign indebtedness. Moreover, the former Czechoslovakia adopted the most radical and rapid programme of microeconomic transformation, through a mass privatization plan, although that was the country in which the central government had stronger control over enterprises. Valuable insights on these apparent incongruities, which make generalizations troublesome, are gained when the origin, formulation and implementation of reform programmes are analysed through the eyes of persons directly involved in the process. In fact, from the answers of Balcerowicz and Klaus it becomes evident that the essentials of the programmes could not have differed substantially, even though the initial conditions diverged.

Political conflicts grew rapidly in the three countries soon after the launching of the reforms, but the relationship between changing political support and economic developments remains unclear. In Poland, the defeat at the elections in 1993 of the parties which had supported reforms since their inception took place in a context of economic recovery and in the very country that has experienced the strongest rebound in output. In the former Czechoslovakia, political conflict culminated in the split of the country at the end of 1992, and the political pressures on the Hungarian government did not abate, and led to a political reversal in the election of May 1994. We hope that the conversations with the reformers may provide the reader with the elements to understand these questions better.

These conversations can provide an analytical window on the perceptions of the actors concerned, on how they evaluated and solved the problems that they faced, reacting to ever-changing circumstances. Although, as stressed above, the particular economic and political conditions distinguish one country's experience from that of others, we believe that the self-examination of policy makers, and the questioning of their own considerations, motivations and reactions, may indeed provide insights and lessons for other countries undergoing similar processes. It was in this spirit that we posed our last question to each of the reformers, requesting them to share with their colleagues in other reforming countries their most important piece of advice.

This project was carried out while the two authors were at the staff of the World Bank. All the interpretations, conclusions and implications in this volume are the authors' own and should not be attributed either to the World Bank (or any of its affiliated institutions) or to the institutions to which the authors are at present affiliated.

The authors are very grateful to the World Bank for support and partial financing, and to their many former colleagues in the Country Economic Department of the Bank. In particular, they wish to thank L. Summers and N. Birdsall for backing the concept of this volume and for their encouragement; A. Gelb for his continuous support and his many suggestions; T. Bayuk, R. Hirschler and L. MacDonald for valuable editorial assistance; and S. Kapur for administrative assistance. They also wish to recognize the Argentinean economist Juan Carlos de Pablo who published in 1980 a volume of interviews with Argentinean policy makers (*La Economia que yo Hice* – or, roughly, 'Economic policy as I made it') from which the concept for this book was derived. Their greatest indebtness, however, is with Messrs Balcerowicz, Bod and Klaus for having found time in their very busy schedules to agree to participate in this project, for their enthusiasm and cooperation, and, above all, for their friendly and open attitude.

1. Personal Formation and the Supporting Environment

This first section describes elements of the early personal and intellectual development of Leszek Balcerowicz of Poland, Peter Bod of Hungary, and Václav Klaus of Czechoslovakia. The period covered here extends until the initiation of reforms and covers their formative years, tracking their transition from research or academia to government policy making. In particular, these discussions touch on their respective academic training and their exposure to western economics, be it through formal training, travel abroad, personal contacts, or access to literature. Most important, the reformers recount here elements that shaped their thinking about economics.

All three men received formative training in economics during distinctively liberal periods in their respective countries and were exposed to western economic thinking and literature well before the reforms started. Leszek Balcerowicz studied at the erstwhile Faculty of Foreign Trade in Warsaw during the first part of the 1970s; in addition, he received an MBA from St. John's University in the USA; he then obtained his PhD in Poland in 1975. Peter Bod began his university training in economics immediately after the introduction of the New Economic Mechanism by János Kádár in 1968 and the subsequent hesitant opening up of the economy and the reorientation of the economic sciences towards the market. Václav Klaus, after finishing his undergraduate degree at the Prague School of Economics in 1963, continued his graduate work at the Institute of Economics of the Czechoslovak Academy of Sciences, a relatively liberal institution where the famous Czechoslovak economic reforms of the late 1960s and, indeed, the Prague Spring originated.

In addition, of course, the direction of their respective careers as well as of their thinking was defined to a great extent by the political circumstances in which they lived. For example, Václav Klaus's career as an economist at the Academy of Sciences in Prague was abruptly terminated when he was dismissed as an 'anti-socialist force'. Since the Warsaw Pact invasion crushed the Prague Spring movement in 1968, the Czechoslovak regime has been the most repressive police state of the three, forcing any reformist intellectual movement underground. Klaus, whose graduate work focused on non-socialist economies, was critical even of the 'third way' thinking that characterized the Prague Spring movement. Those who were proponents of the 'third way' tried to create an alternative to both socialism and capitalism, a 'socialism with a human face'. Klaus, along with the Club of Young Economists which he founded in 1968, was critical of any programme that did not advocate a significant movement towards market reforms. After his dismissal from the Academy in 1970, Klaus occupied various positions in the Czechoslovak State Bank until 1986, and in 1987 he was allowed to return to the Academy of Sciences, where he became head of the Department for Macroeconomic Policy at the Institute of Forecasting.

The Polish state allowed much more academic freedom than the Czechoslovak one, even though the relationship between the communist state and Polish civil society has been historically an antagonistic one, particularly during the long period of martial law in the 1980s. Like Václav Klaus, Leszek Balcerowicz of Poland did not believe in the efficiency of the socialist centrally planned economy; however, given the political conditions at the time, he did not forecast any drastic change. 'I did believe that a comprehensive economic reform was ruled out by geopolitical restraints,' Balcerowicz explains, 'but there was still enough room for economic improvement within the existing constraints to make it worth attempting.' As a researcher at the Institute of Economic Development of the Central School of Planning and Statistics, and as a party member, Balcerowicz enjoyed relative academic freedom, including travel and teaching in the west; he left the party with the imposition of martial law in 1981.

Under János Kádár, with the introduction of the New Economic Mechanism in 1968, Hungary's official position shifted towards a greater openness to the market and a pro-gramme of careful economic reform that characterized the country's economic policy for the next twenty years. The implementation of market socialism as an alternative to full-scale socialist planning, while tentative, allowed for a degree of state tolerance for certain sectors of Hungarian society that did not exist elsewhere. This included tolerance of the Academy, as in Poland. 'After the mid-seventies,' Bod recounts, 'it was not assumed that a university student was a Marxist - so long as he did not openly declare that he was one.' After completing his studies at the university, Peter Bod worked as a researcher at the Institute of Economic Planning affiliated to the National Planning Office, where he worked for seventeen years and travelled to the west as a scholar and consultant. Bod describes the variety of views - not all of them explicit - regarding the party and the market economy that existed at the Institute, where only half of the researchers were party members. By the late 1980s, this tolerance had increased, as official studies were being conducted by a growing number of researchers, including

Bod and his department, on the necessity of developing market institutions, as the economic decline in Hungary demonstrated the exhaustion of the Hungarian alternative.

Whereas in Hungary Bod can describe the debates held among groups at the (Economic) Mechanism Department that he headed, and the studies which his department was commissioned to conduct by the Hungarian state itself, in Poland and Czechoslovakia discussions on market reform were held in much more informal contexts: both Balcerowicz in Poland and Klaus in Czechoslovakia set up informal groups that debated free market issues and reforms.

In Poland, Balcerowicz founded and directed a group of eleven young economists in 1978 who worked together on a project for economic reform in Poland. Balcerowicz describes the aims of what later became known simply as the Balcerowicz group: 'We set ourselves the following task: given certain constraints, prepare a blueprint of an economic system which would bring about a maximum gain of efficiency as compared to the existing one.' The groups came out public with the project in November 1980 and continued to work together on the blueprint until 1981 when, with the imposition of martial law, it became more of an academic seminar on economic issues; the group continued in this fashion until 1989, when a number of its members followed Balcerowicz into government.

In Czechoslovakia, Václav Klaus organized and chaired an informal monthly seminar which criticized the existing centrally planned economy and discussed issues concerning the free market. The seminars began in 1980 and continued for six years, and its contributions were published and circulated, so that, as Klaus explains, 'A whole generation of Czech economists considered them their economic education. The Czechoslovak economic (and not only economic) reform was immensely influenced by the thinking and discussions of our group.'

Could you please elaborate on your professional background? Tell us briefly about your formal (academic) as well as informal professional formation. During your years of study, did you specialize in economics or in some other field?

BALCEROWICZ: I graduated with distinction in 1970 from the Faculty of Foreign Trade of the Warsaw School of Planning and Statistics (now the Warsaw School of Economics). This faculty was probably the most western-oriented faculty of economics among the Comecon countries in the late 1960s, and was certainly much less rigid and orthodox than those in the former Soviet Union or the former GDR. For example, the Polish textbook for International Economics was not very different from the well-known book by Kindleberger used in the west.

Between September 1972 and January 1974, I studied Business Administration at St. John's University in New York, from which I graduated with Beta Gamma Sigma. Within the MBA programme I specialized in economics. This was an opportunity for me to get better acquainted with western macro- and microeconomics. I was also reading widely on the economics of technological change while working on my doctoral dissertation. One of my favourite subjects was probability calculus.

In 1974 I returned to the Central School of Planning and Statistics where I taught international economics while intensively working on my doctorate, which dealt with the social costs of speeding up product innovations. I defended it in 1975; a radically enlarged version was published as a book in Poland in 1979.

Since the early days of my academic career, I've had a feeling that 'institutions matter', that is that behind the differences in economic performance there are first of all differences in institutional arrangements or, in other words, in economic systems. This led to my interest in the economic reform of the socialist system. There were two considerations here. First, I did not have, except perhaps only for my early student years, many illusions that any socialist economy (as defined by non-private property rights) could be as efficient as a competitive capitalist economy. Second, I believed that such an economy was ruled out by geopolitical constraints, but that there was still enough room for economic improvement within these constraints to make it worth attempting. This was, I think, an important consideration in my joining the Polish United Workers' Party in 1969 and in accepting a job in the economic department of the party institute between 1978 and May 1980. (I left the party immediately after the introduction of martial law in December 1981 when I returned from a short conference abroad.)

After the introduction of martial law, I returned practically full-time to academic life, except for participating in editing one of the underground magazines. I conducted a seminar on economic theory and economic systems at the Institute for Economic Development at the Central School of Planning and Statistics, where I continued to work. The members of the original 'Balcerowicz group' [see below] participated in this seminar along with some other people. Many of them entered into government service with myself in 1989.

In my academic work I focused on the institutional aspects of economic issues. I have written articles dealing with, among other things, the issues of property rights, including the importance of private ownership for organizational dynamics and technical change. I also compared various economic systems (centrally planned, 'reformed', and capitalist) from the point of view of their technological innovativeness. The conclusion was clear: no system can match the technological dynamics of the free-enterprise economy.

The main result of this period was the book *Economic Systems: Elements of Comparative Analysis*, completed in 1988. It focused, first of all, on some basic general issues, for example the role of institutional versus cultural (psychosocial) factors in shaping a country's economic performance, and, second, on the efficiency of coordination under alternative economic systems. There I took issue with János Kornai's explanation of shortages in terms of an enterprise's 'soft budget constraint'. I maintained instead that the most important determinants are administratively controlled prices and inflexible supply, the latter due to central control over the economy and a rigid foreign trade system.

The issue of coordination was related to the problem of stabilizing an economy under high inflation or hyperinflation. Hence I was interested in the stabilization programmes of the Latin American countries. I drew two lessons from the literature on this subject: first, hyperinflation cannot be reduced in a gradual manner, so a kind of discontinuous or 'shock' therapy is needed; second, this therapy should be introduced as soon as possible, for the longer one tolerates hyperinflation, the more difficult and costly it is to get rid of it, given the stronger formal and informal retrospective indexation.

In the spring of 1989, I wrote a paper on the conclusions to be drawn from the experience of various economies, and from economic theory, regarding the changes desirable in the Polish economy. I did not bother to consider at that time whether or not these conclusions were politically realistic, and I had no idea that a few months later I would be in charge of the Polish economic stabilization and transformation. But the conclusions were rather similar to the main points of the economic programme adopted in the autumn of

1989: rapid liberalization of prices, tough macroeconomic policy, convertibility of the Polish zloty, the liberalization of the foreign trade regime, the fastest possible privatization, and so on.

BOD: I completed high school in 1969 in what was then the second largest city in the country, in the centre of the heavy industry region, Miskolc. At the secondary school I attended the humanities class: that is, I took Latin (and, of course, Russian), although my favourite subject was history. With the approach of finals, however, I devoted my energies to studying mathematics and physics, as I intended to apply to the technical university since there was no arts faculty at Miskolc at the time. Finally, I took a different decision and applied for admission to the University of Economics in Budapest.

My career choice was influenced by a number of circumstances. My parents were grammar school teachers; my father, the late Andor Bod, was sentenced to one and a half years in prison for his public role in the events of the 1956 revolution and was afterwards banned from practising his profession. It amounted to a minor miracle that my mother was able to maintain the family and educate both my sister and myself on a teacher's miserable pay. The argument in favour of a technical career was that, owing to the relatively small number of applicants, my 'wrong origin' would not have mattered so much. And, of course, living with one's parents during one's university years is the least costly arrangement. Moreover, given that 'socialist' higher education was geared to regulating the supply of graduates, after graduation no one had to reckon with difficulties in finding employment: if you got an engineering degree, you were certain to find a place at a factory; if it was a degree in history, then at a grammar school. Seeing their humiliatingly low pay, I did not want to become a teacher, even though I have always liked teaching and, in various forms, I have in fact been teaching since I was a teenager (coaching others) to this very day (as university lecturer).

My decision to study economics was surprising only to my immediate family since on both my father's and my mother's side we had mainly teachers and clergymen in the family. Otherwise, it was a logical choice at a time when, with the introduction of the New Economic Mechanism in 1968, all of a sudden new vistas opened up in the economic sciences. Until then, the economist and, to some extent, the lawyer, were among the tolerated professions. From 1968, however, the careful and hesitant political opening-up towards a market economy required more economists.

Thus, following a year of mandatory military service, I was admitted to the Karl Marx University of Economics in Budapest. The courses to be taken in the first year were the same for all; afterwards we could specialize. With my strong academic performance, I had numerous choices (except for special subjects in diplomatic training, characteristically reserved for the children of families deemed to be 'trustworthy'). I chose the prestigious 'national economic planning' as my specialty; here one could obtain a degree after five years of study (in contrast to the four or four and a half years in the microeconomics faculties); this faculty was regarded as the most demanding, with training provided in mathematics, languages and general economic sciences. Later, in the third year, the opportunity was provided for further specialization: I then chose 'enterprise modelling'. The 'national economic planning' specialty guaranteed more quantitative subjects and economic theory and, with the new specialty, I could acquire a thorough knowledge of accounting, operations research and some marketing and legal knowledge instead of focusing on more ideological subjects.

In 1977, I obtained a PhD with the quantitative analysis of the typical growth strategies of industrial enterprises and then, in 1986, the Hungarian Scientific Academy conferred on me the degree of 'candidate' (there is no equivalent of this degree in the English-speaking world). My thesis – which a year later was also published in book form – analysed the functions of the state in a modern mixed economy, including also the economic theory debates on the role of the state in Western Europe and the experiments with nationalization and privatization in the early 1980s. Not long after graduation I began to teach at the Department of Industrial Operations Management, which gave me an opportunity to supplement macroeconomic research (my full-time occupation) with the cultivation of microeconomics. When later, by caprice of history, I became Minister of Industry and Trade, I was able to make good use of my basic training in macro- and microeconomics. In 1986 I was appointed head of the Department of Economic Control. By then the Institute had a new leadership: the new director and his deputy were not party members. (That was not typical even in the Hungary of 1988.) In any case, I was also not pressured to join the establishment party.

KLAUS: I finished my studies at the Prague School of Economics in 1963; my special field of studies was 'foreign trade'. The whole school was run fully according to the tenets of Marxist political economy, but studying foreign trade was something exceptional. You were forced to study foreign languages and you were supposed to be able to communicate with your partners in the western business world, therefore some more pragmatic economic issues were part of the curriculum.

Immediately after finishing my undergraduate studies I continued in my postgraduate studies in the Institute of

Economics of the Czechoslovak Academy of Sciences in Prague. The Institute was more or less a research institution where the famous Czechoslovak economic reform of the late 1960s and also the Prague Spring of 1968 originated. In this respect and at that time, it was, relatively speaking, a very liberal institution compared with the rest of the communist world.

I worked in the department which was supposed to study western, non-socialist economies and to criticize non-Marxist economic theories, which in reality meant to study them. I got my graduate degree in February 1968 and continued to do my research in the institute until the purges that followed the Soviet invasion in August 1968.

During your formative years, were you active in students' movements? Were you involved in any formal or informal political activity? Were you an active member of any political organization?

BALCEROWICZ: As a student, I was a member and treasurer of a student organization at my faculty. The Faculty of Foreign Trade organized the international East-West Student Seminars. This was an opportunity to meet people from various countries, both eastern and western. I remember presenting a paper at this seminar in 1969 on the relationship between economic reform and East-West trade. After graduating in 1970 I started to work as an assistant in the Department of International Economics of the Central School of Planning and Statistics.

As I mentioned earlier, I was a member of the Polish United Workers' Party from 1969 to 1981, until the introduction of martial law in December of that year.

BOD: In countries with sound histories, student movements mean training-fields, facing challenges that clarify one's views and, for the interested and the ambitious, opportunities to enter public life. In the sovietized states, the only youth movement apart from the illegal or marginal groupings (such as church communities) was called upon to serve the 'cadre replacement' of the communist party. The mentality of this movement in Hungary is hard to define, although its name was highly suggestive in including, as a remarkable exception, the adjective 'communist' at a time when the communist party did not dare to appear under any but stage names (Workers' Party, Socialist Workers' Party). After 1956 not even the most conformist member of the establishment party would have dared to say that the people could regard communism as their own. This was particularly true of the young. At the universities and workplaces, the youth organization functioned partly as the most practical leisure-time organization (for example, organizing sports events, dances, and so forth) and partly as an institution that represented interests. Those who wanted to go into party politics could, by taking on a post in the extensive bureaucracy of the youth organization, quickly catch the eye of the personnel managers of the communist party.

I was a member of this youth organization throughout my years at secondary school, in military service, at university, and even for a few years afterwards. On the whole, however, I can say that I was not into organized politics.

It should be noted here – all the more so, as what I say may also be of political interest – that, not being a resident of Budapest, I did not move to a 'normal' student hostel, but to a so-called special college – something in between a student hotel and a college. The student had to perform regular academic work, take on special courses, and report to the other students on his or her findings. This selection procedure guaranteed that, over and above the otherwise not too intensive academic studies, we were also introduced to the world of organized research work. And what was politically interesting in this was that from this college - these students, no doubt, were more ambitious than the average student - there emerged quite a number of the representatives of the political scene later on. It is also true that this elite has represented many hues in the political spectrum and has done so until this day.

KLAUS: I was not active in any kind of students' movements and I was not a member of any political organization. In 1968 I founded the 'Club of young economists' (with some 300 members), where I tried to criticize the intermediate 'third way' thinking of the Prague Spring period and argued for real economic reforms of the type we are able to realize just now.

Before joining the government, at the beginning of the reform process, did you have any previous experience in government administration at a senior or managerial level? Did you work with previous governments in any advisory capacity? Did you have the chance to discuss economic issues with government officials of previous administrations?

BALCEROWICZ: My only experience of working in the government's administration was a part-time job in the secretariat of the Council for Technical Change in the Planning Commission in 1976-78. But this wasn't at a senior level. As a leader of the group of young economists, I was also consulted in 1981 by the government's secretariat on economic reform. The main issue was the introduction of the two-tier banking sector in Poland, which I proposed in the group's report on the economic reform. This proposal wasn't at that time accepted; the two-tier banking system was introduced in Poland only in early 1989 by the last Party government.

BOD: It is well known how the previous regime monopolized any say in matters of government. Still, there were some differences: whereas, as far as the press was concerned, absolute control was asserted, economic matters were conducted more in the open. After graduating I could have stayed at the university (to teach political economy) and I also had an offer at an institute of applied research (to do operations research). Yet by chance I learned that there was a vacancy at the research institute of the National Planning Office (NPO) – the Institute for Economic Planning (IEP). I joined the IEP as a researcher in September 1975 and continued to work there until I was invited to join the first Hungarian government to be elected democratically after many decades, in May 1990.

Perhaps I may be allowed a little detour about research institutes. Economic research in the former so-called socialist countries was conducted in three types of institutions. First, there were university departments – far removed from any decision making, their time shared between teaching and research, and at low salaries. Second, there were the research institutes of the Scientific Academy: also quite far removed from real life, but as full-time researchers their staff worked under better conditions, with more foreign contacts. The third type was the research institutes operating under state agencies and ministries. In Hungary, every economic ministry had at least one research institute. At these institutes researchers had better contacts with government decision making; they were, in general, adequately informed but, in addition to research into their 'favourite' topic, they also had specific tasks to do at short notice (ranging from quick analyses to writing the minister's May

Day speech). After the change to democracy the new economic decision makers who took over were recruited from these institutes as well as from the Academy and university departments.

To return to my own professional activities: the Institute worked mainly for the NPO. At first, my task consisted of analysing the links between the two levels of planning – state and enterprises. The staff members of the Institute were also frequently involved in the work of the numerous working parties and committees organized by the government. Although I have no knowledge of any acute problem that would have been solved through a committee, the insight into the workings of the state (that is, party) leadership was not without lessons for a young researcher.

Owing to my low rank, I hardly ever met members of the top leadership in those years. Following my publications, I began to get assignments from the top managers of the NPO. After 1968, the National Planning Office of Hungary functioned less and less as a planning office and much more as an economic ministry. Matters that could not be assigned sectorally were under the scope of its authority: regional policy and structural policy, as well as the strategic issues – growth, inflation, borrowing – and the internal criticism of the sectoral ministries.

There was one more channel through which the profession was able to communicate with the decision makers: the Hungarian Economic Society (HES). For a good decade, I was secretary of the Macroeconomic Section, which required organizing lectures and discussions. One of the main events was the lectures by domestic researchers or foreign economists visiting Hungary. This provided an opportunity for official economic politicians to present current ideas and conceptions and to test their reception by the professional community through the questions asked and the ensuing debate.

KLAUS: After being forced to leave the Academy of Sciences in 1970 (as a leading 'anti-socialist force'), I was lucky to find a job in the Central Bank of Czechoslovakia where I spent – in different positions – seventeen years, until 1987. I slowly moved in the Bank from very irrelevant positions through econometric modelling in the computer centre to something that might be called an 'advisory' position. The Central Bank in a centrally planned economy is an institution comparable to any ministry, and I had, therefore, plenty of chances to discuss economic issues with government officials of previous administrations.

In the course of your formal education, were you exposed in any meaningful way to western-type economics? How did you became familiar with western economics concepts? Was literature on 'market' economics available in any form (textbooks, articles, etc.)? Were market economics concepts discussed freely in formal or informal student gatherings? What was your view about these issues at that time?

BALCEROWICZ: The Faculty of Foreign Trade of the Warsaw School of Economics provided relatively good exposure to international economics. Of importance were also my MBA studies at St. John's University. While working on the doctorate, I became familiar with the western literature on technical change including that on the institutional determinants of the pace and structure of technological innovations (Schumpeter, Schmookler, Rosenberg, Gomulka, Mansfield and others). My interests in the institutional aspects of economic activity, related to my interests in economic reform, had led me, in the 1980s, to the literature on property rights, law and economics and on comparative economic systems. I became familiar with both the Anglo-Saxon

publications on these subjects and the West German literature (W. Eucken, P. Hensel). I studied in depth the 'socialist
calculation debate' in the western literature and have a fairly
good knowledge of the works of Lange, Mises, Hayek and
Schumpeter, and also of newer works (Alchian, Williamson,
Pejovitsch, Ward and others).

Because of my interest in the problems of economic
coordination and the related issues of the shortage economy,
I studied the questions of inflation, recession, and stabilization in the market economies. As a matter of fact, I have
translated into Polish some western publications (J. Hicks,
N. Kaldor, H. Johnson, S. Weintraub, H. J. Grossman).
These were published as a collection of essays by the Research Institute of the Problems of Contemporary Capitalism
in Warsaw in 1976.

I have also been interested in the experience of the real
world in market economies. I was especially attracted to the
cases of radical policy shifts leading to what were called,
after the event, 'economic miracles'. So I studied in depth
the experience of South Korea, as a visiting scholar at the
Institute of Development Studies at the University of Sussex
for five months in 1985. I also spent, thanks to the Friedrich
Ebert Stiftung, three months in West Germany in the autumn
of 1988, studying Ludwig Erhard's reforms of 1948 and the
subsequent developments.

Finally, it is worth mentioning that the library at the
Warsaw School of Economics offered free access to the
most important western economics journals. I've been making use of this possibility by trying to keep abreast of new
developments in the western economic literature. I've also
been interested in the problems of the psychology of motivation and in social psychology (for example, the theory of
cognitive dissonance, the theory of achievement motivation),
for I believed and still believe that economic theory should

be built on strong psychological foundations. In this regard I have a great appreciation for the work of Herbert Simon. I became familiar with psychology of decision making, as very well presented by the Polish psychologist Jozef Kozielecki.

BOD: As the vast majority of the Hungarian economists graduated from the University of Economics, then named after Karl Marx, today named after the city of Budapest, the question of whether economists could have had access to modern economic thinking is important, quite irrespective of any personal considerations.

Curriculums consisted of two groups of subjects: the ideological and the professional ones. Ideological subjects had to be taken by everyone. These subjects ('scientific socialism'; the history of the workers' movement; philosophy; political economy) made up the smaller – and over time, decreasing – part of university and college education. Especially after the economic reform of 1968, the share of professional subjects increased and standards also improved somewhat at the University of Economics. With the re-discovery of market concepts, even the teaching of the ideological subjects, such as political economy, became more lively: Marx's critique of capitalism can be taught in a narrow-minded, hidebound way, but also in a meaningful way, with sensitivity to the problems.

A few specific circumstances greatly helped me to become acquainted with modern economics. For instance, the fact that quantitative macro- and microeconomic subjects were taught in the mainstream was widely accepted in the west. There was no separate Marxist operations research, probability calculation, microeconomics. Secondly, self-training and regular research work quickly helped me past the books available in Hungarian (which obviously, in the main, reflected the official economic approach of the time). Those who could read foreign languages could have access to western economic literature without administrative difficulties. Thirdly: after the mid-1970s, foreign scholarships and grants began to be available, first for young lecturers and researchers and then also for students.

Through the international organization of economists and finance students (AIESEC), in 1973 I spent two months in Finland, working as a trainee on statistics at the Agricultural Research Institute. The time I spent there was very useful. We had to face the fact that it was hard to understand the concepts used in the west. Also, the way in which a human community and workplace functioned under democratic conditions had a great impression on the world-view of the trainee.

In general, Hungarians – and especially students – travelled around a great deal in the 1970s. Because of passport and financial constraints, the target country of the 1960s was mainly Poland but later more and more people visited western countries as well. I also spent a month in Germany together with some of my university friends, earning the money needed for the trip doing illegàl work. On the basis of such experiences, the interested Hungarian citizen with some education could gain an impression of several aspects of a market economy: mainly of the habits of consumption, less regarding issues such as employment, and obviously much less concerning matters such as the micro-mechanisms of community life (family life, religion, political preferences).

KLAUS: In my undergraduate years western economics was unknown to me, but after entering the Academy of Sciences in September 1964, nothing other than 'western' economics was the object of my studies. I wanted to study economics and there is no alternative economic science. It was sometimes difficult to get hold of western literature but, as always in economics, if you look for something there are always transaction costs to get it. Therefore, 'searching' was the process whereby we could get journals and books. The costs of searching were non-zero, but the marginal contribution after reading (and the consumer's surplus) was enormous. But, of course, there was never a textbook in the Czech language available – the first one came out in 1990. In the sixties a group of young graduate students founded a seminar (without a teacher, because there were no teachers of that kind) based on Samuelson's sixth edition of his famous textbook. I was doing that again, as a teacher, between 1985 and 1989.

Before the beginning of the reforms, were you acquainted with western economists, intellectuals or politicians; did you have any professional contacts with them? Did you participate in conferences, symposiums, or any other gatherings of western economists?

BALCEROWICZ: Since 1976 I've been in close touch with the Hungarian 'reform economists' (for example, T. Bauer, M. Tardos, M. Laki, A. Soos) as Hungary was widely considered, until about the middle of the 1980s, to be the model of the politically possible economic reform. I was familiar with and appreciated the works of János Kornai.

Since the early 1980s I stayed in close contact with a group of West German liberal economists – pupils of the late P. Hensel in Marburg, now working at various West German universities (for example, Alfred Schuller in Marburg, Dieter Cassel in Duisburg). I participated in two of their annual seminars, organized in Radein (northern Italy), dedicated to some selected aspects of comparative economics. As mentioned earlier, I spent three months in Marburg in 1988 studying the West German 'Wirtschafswunder' [economic miracle] under Ludwig Erhard.

During my stay as a visiting scholar at the Institute for Development Studies at the University of Sussex in 1985, I had the opportunity to establish good contacts with a number of researchers, such as Raphael Kaplinsky and Gordon White.

Since 1980, I have also been in close touch with British economists of Polish origin, especially Jacek Rostowski, Stanislaw Gomulka and Edward Szczepanik. Gomulka and Rostowski later became my advisers when I was in the government. Since 1985 I have been in touch with people in the Economics Department of the Staffordshire Polytechnic in Stoke-on-Trent, Britain, especially with Iraj Hashi, with whom I organized a regular exchange of students. As a matter of fact, it was to this Polytechnic that I was supposed to come for one year in the autumn of 1989 to lecture on, among other things, comparative economic systems, socialist economics and post-Keynesian economics.

I've been in regular contact since 1986 with Pavel Pelikan, a Czech working at the Industrial Institute for Economic and Social Research in Stockholm. We share an interest in the issues of institutional dynamics. It was at this institute, after my lecture in 1986, that I met Wladyslaw Brzeski, a Polish specialist in real-estate economics, who emigrated to the west some twenty years ago. He joined my team in 1989 as my adviser on the financial aspects of housing and real estate and eventually settled down for good in Poland.

I have also had some good friends among the economists in India at the New Delhi University (for example Amitabh Kundu), where I went on a lecture tour in 1987. One of the insights I gained there was that widespread poverty pushes some well-meaning and intelligent people to search for quick solutions, which results in a demand for ever-increasing state intervention, hence an over-regulated and inefficient economy.

A study tour in the US organized by the US Information Agency in June 1988 gave me the opportunity to get personally acquainted with a number of American economists such as Abraham Bergson, Steve Pejovitsch, and David Granick.

BOD: Before answering the question, a few words should be said about the concept of 'reform'. For me it is evident that whatever has been taking place in the former Soviet empire since 1989 goes far beyond what could still be termed 'reform'. The matter at hand is not the reformation of the economic-social system any more: what is going on is a change of system. Perhaps the excessive use of the term 'reform' can be attributed to the fact that the changes in the countries showing the most progress, in view of their specific circumstances, did not appear in the guise of a revolution and were not accompanied by violence. What is more, in Hungary, for instance, no great outbursts of public sentiment accompanied the change in the political structure, and within it the change in the forms of the state – the institutions, the symbols. The situation had become so ripe for winding up such a dead-end way of development that the outgoing government and the communist party adopted right away a number of 'reform measures' that any new government would also have taken. This could be attributed partly to the fact that the old elite wished to implement the inevitable changes, since they could not be avoided any longer, in a way beneficial to their own interests, and partly to the fact that, in view of the approaching elections, they tried to anticipate voter sentiments. This, however, will not alter the fact that the term to be used for the changes taking place in the political structure, the legal and institutional policy after 1990 is not 'reform' but 'systemic change'. Whenever I use the term 'reform', I refer to the careful, hesitant, stop-go reform course followed in Hungary from the late 1960s until the end of the 1980s.

The end of the 1980s found the leaders of the Hungarian community of economists in an ambiguous situation. With freer research conditions and the continuous expansion of international contacts, it was not only the representatives of official scholarship (who, by the very nature of the matter, generally were close to the political leadership) who could attend conferences abroad, but also the second-level scholars. I, for instance, after an unsuccessful application some time before, won a scholarship for four months at the Institute of Economics in Copenhagen, Denmark. (I could not help wondering at the success of this application: I won that scholarship in the very year when, for the first time, the questionnaire did not include the question about the criminal record of one's father.) Later, through the contacts of the Institute and personal acquaintances, I made study trips to the Netherlands (University of Tilburg), where I also lectured (Research Institute for Management Science, Delft), made presentations at conferences in the United States, Turkey, France, Yugoslavia, Finland, and so on.

Many of my agile colleagues with good language skills had the opportunity to attend conferences abroad. Visiting professors also came to Hungary more frequently; in fact, foreign students also began to turn up from the second half of the 1980s at the Budapest University of Economics (just as at the medical and the technical schools.)

Many of Hungary's so-called 'leading economists', who had monopolized western contacts for a long time, progressed, at best, to the stage of promoting the reform of the existing system or simply of acquiring the terminology of reform. However, in comparison with the representatives of other East European countries, even a polished Hungarian Stalinist could pass himself off quite well in western circles. This may have caused misunderstandings later, during the period immediately preceding the change in regimes, when western consultants discussed important issues with already discredited individuals, frequently involving them in their joint projects.

This, however, applied to only a minority of the 'leading economists'. Most of them were true reformers, that is - in the sense explained above - they worked on the improvement of the specific Hungarian form of socialism, frequently coming into close contact with pragmatic officials of the communist party. The Academy of Sciences had never been able to contact the top political leadership so easily as during the last two reform-communist governments. Some of the 'leading reform economists' lost a specific market: earlier, a great deal could be written about the link between plan and market, that is, about reformed socialism as a kind of third way. The economics of market socialism were developed almost to perfection when, all of a sudden, socialism itself fell apart. Perhaps a great part of the lack of enthusiasm with which many in the economists' opinion-shaping community responded to the change in regimes is due to factors such as these. Also, the new system requires modern knowledge or, at least, a good capacity for learning: a great deal - indeed, almost everything - of 'socialist economics' had to be forgotten and a great deal - likewise, almost everything - had to be learnt anew. Some of the 'reform economists' have been able to achieve this; others have preferred to put on fastidious airs.

Coming back to my own career: from the mid-1980s, I studied and worked abroad more and more. Through personal contacts, I became a member of an expert team that visited Ghana several times in 1986–87 to help reorganize the economic planning tasks of the Ministry of Finance, for the UNDP. I also gained an insight into the functioning of major international organizations (UN, IMF, World Bank), and into the world of aid programmes and international assistance. Also through personal research contacts, I spent the summer terms at Portland State University (Oregon, USA), where I gave three courses each term in 1987 and 1988.

KLAUS: I had an opportunity to spend five months on a postgraduate course devoted to the problems of economic development in ISVE, Naples, Italy, in 1966, and to spend a spring term at Cornell University, Ithaca, NY, in 1969. But from the 1970s until the second half of the 1980s, people like me were not allowed to travel to the west. In some respects it was 'lost' time, but in another sense it was a perfect time to study, to prepare oneself for the challenge which might come. And it did come. My first participation in an economic conference in the west was in October 1988, after almost twenty years. In the meantime I had the chance to meet friends in Czechoslovakia and, in addition, to participate in conferences and seminars in Poland and Hungary where it was possible to meet western economists.

In the years prior to reforms, did you carry out your professional work as a team (formal or informal) or did you work mainly as an independent technician? If you worked mainly in a team, what were the issues on economic reform that were discussed? Was there a consensus on market economies? Were any general plans for economic reform being drawn up or discussed?

BALCEROWICZ: In 1978 at the Research Institute for Economic Development of the Warsaw School of Economics, I formed and directed an informal group of young economists to work on a project of economic reform in Poland. This group, which became widely known as 'the Balcerowicz group', had eleven members and we worked quite intensively in 1978-81. We set ourselves the following task: given certain constraints (the impossibility of privatizing the state sector, of leaving Comecon, and of abolishing the rule of the PUWP), prepare a blueprint of an economic system which would bring about a maximum gain in efficiency compared to the existing one. The result of our intensive work (we met almost every week for more than two years) was a thorough discussion of many important issues, including how to prevent workers in self-managed enterprises from consuming profits, what instruments of indirect control the state should have in the economy, how to build a two-tier banking system, what powers a local government body should have). The overall result was two reports, which I wrote on behalf of the group. The first described the proposed economic system, which might have been called an incomplete and non-private market economy, and the second dealt with the issue of transition to this system.

When in August 1980 'Solidarity' came into being, there was a great demand for 'social' – that is, unofficial – proposals for economic reform, and the 'Balcerowicz group' project was recognized by many as the most radical and complete. It generated wide interest among members of 'Solidarity', which for myself, as for many other Poles, was important as a broad-based movement for reform and not so much as a trade union. In March 1981 I was elected vice-chairman of the Polish Economic Association with responsibility for economic reform (I resigned from this function in December 1982 because I believed that, in the situation created by martial law, radical economic reform had little chance of being pursued). From 1981 onwards, the task force on economic reform became something of a seminar on the basic problems of economic systems (that is, property rights, the proper role of the state in the economy, shortages and inflation) and continued at a lesser pace until democratization in 1989.

I entered government service in September 1989 with some members of the original group or persons who joined it later, such as Dabrowski and Kavalec. The formation of the government in late August and early September of 1989 was done in such a way that, having accepted the task of directing Poland's economic programme, I had much say in who should get the economic portfolios. Thanks to this, some of these functions went to liberal-minded people. The same was true of the second government, created in early 1991.

There was no doubt among the members of the economic team that a radical economic change was imperative. The views about the general directions of the reform were shared partly because they were discussed beforehand, during the seminars in my institute. The economic programme was arrived at by successive proposals and bargaining, and the first version was more or less ready within two weeks, by late September 1989.

BOD: After the mid-1970s, the Hungarian regime became increasingly soft – and cynical. The government promised little and demanded little. Thus, it was not assumed that a university student was a Marxist – so long as he did not openly declare that he was one. Also, at the research institute that I joined in 1975, people with very different views worked together. About half of my colleagues – and all the leaders, without exception, at that time – were members of the party.

My department occupied the most interesting position in the Institute. Its name – Economic Mechanism (later: Economic Control) Department – reflected the prevailing conceptual uncertainty, and this may have been deliberate. The term 'mechanism' is not particularly meaningful, unless it is used as the opposite of 'plan'. According to the classic Stalinist political approach, the communists know what is to be done and do it. Classic Stalinist policy, however, failed in a far-reaching way in Hungary in 1956: the ordinary people spectacularly demonstrated they had enough of the Plan. The term 'mechanism' points to the self-organizing capacity of the economy, to the laws of economics, and also to the fact that not everything needs to be planned. The term made a real career for itself when the Hungarian economic reform of 1968, opening up somewhat towards the market, was officially named the New Economic Mechanism (NEM).

The Mechanism Department of the Institute dealt with institutional issues (the organization of state administration, information flows between the state and the enterprises, as well as matters of economic regulation), and with the objectives and instruments of economic policy. As a result of the wide range of subjects and the small staff, it was rare to have overlaps, thus characteristically we worked on our own. But the debates within the Institute and the informal discussions within the Department sufficiently revealed the differences in views.

At the turn of 1987 and in 1988 one could already feel that the possibilities of gradual step-by-step reform had by then been exhausted. There were quite a few people at the Institute who had firsthand knowledge of the economy of the Soviet Union. In any case, we had many personal contacts with Soviet colleagues: they loved to come to Hungary, that is, to the 'west'. Most were generally of the view that the changes initiated by Gorbachev would not produce results in the economy. Hungary's growing indebtedness to the west and the dependence of fundamental industries upon a spectacularly decaying Soviet Union – these facts foreshadowed recognition that the peculiar Hungarian 'third way' could not be maintained for long, either in Hungary or elsewhere.

After 1988, events began to speed up, views began to polarize and debates began to be conducted in small groups, rather than involving the Institute as a whole. The department which I headed became one such group. In addition, the state commissioned us to think about what sort of institutions would be required by a market economy.

The first comprehensive study, 'Market-Oriented Economic Policy', was completed in the summer of 1988; in retrospect, it may seem to have been a little naive. Its point of departure was that the political system of parliamentary democracy would take many years, perhaps as much as a decade to implement. Moreover, we did not reckon with the rapid extinction of the CMEA (Comecon). Thus the essence of the recommended economic policy package was: deregulation of the economy (prices, imports, wages, the exchange rate), a strong anti-monopoly stand, encouragement of small business, and 'restructuring' the crisis sectors (steel, coal, agriculture).

At the end of 1988, together with my colleagues, I prepared a study on the development of market institutions, with particular emphasis on the development of the financial system, under the title 'On the Monetization of the Hungarian Economy and the Development of the Banking Institutions'. The main points concerned the underdeveloped state of the securities market, the general inadequacy of the banking institutions, and the monopolistic nature of Hungarian banking.

As far as the economic views of the staff members of the Department were concerned, I could perhaps define them as *institutional* economics based on the heterogeneous background already referred to (Schumpeter, Galbraith, Hayek, and the property rights school, for instance, had a great impact on all of us), accompanied by a strong interest in sociology. At the same time, these young staff members (aged between 28 and 38) were perfectly familiar with the application of quantitative methods, and several of us had the chance of studying and working in functioning market economies and democracies.

KLAUS: At the beginning of the 1980s, I succeeded in organizing a monthly seminar which I chaired and where we had a unique opportunity to discuss a wide range of economic issues. The seminars started in 1980 and were abruptly 'stopped' in January 1986 by the Ministry of the Interior. A whole generation of Czech economists thought of them as their economic education. The contributions to the seminars were published in twelve bulletins. The seminars did not openly discuss the political regime, but the devastating criticism of the existing centrally planned economy, the free market visions of the future, and the critique of the irrelevancy of the official Marxist political economy were presented in a very explicit form. The concepts and ideas of market economy, private property, monetarism (not Keynesianism), Milton Friedman, George Stiegler, the public choice school's criticism of government intervention, disequilibrium macroeconomics, and so forth, were the ideological background of our group. The Czechoslovak economic (and not only economic) reform was immensely influenced by the thinking and discussions of that group.

The general consensus emerging was that to draw up a plan for economic reform is wrong and misplaced. It represents a constructivistic, pseudo-rationalistic thinking. What we need is a *vision* of where we want to go, a *strategy* (not a detailed blueprint!) of how to get there, and finally a basic, elementary *consensus* supporting the reform. The establishment of a market economy was considered to be a more or less spontaneous process which you have to start and have to try to support, but a process which cannot be master-minded from above. The market economy cannot be 'introduced': it must evolve. The preconditions were very simple:

- macroeconomic stability (very cautious monetary and fiscal policies);
- price liberalization;
- foreign trade liberalization and currency convertibility;
- privatization.

No other special plans were seen as necessary.

2. Conceptualizing the Reforms, the Design of the Reform Package and Preconditions for its Implementation

The accounts in the following section pick up the story after the political transition of power in Hungary, Poland and Czechoslovakia, at the time when the reformers were working as policy makers in the government. In the following pages, they discuss the reasoning behind the design of their reform packages prior to their implementation. Their accounts expound two main themes: the identification of the main objectives of the reforms, and the factors that influenced their choice of policies to achieve these objectives. As far as the first theme is concerned, the reformers discuss the aims they had in mind in drawing up their reform programmes. The second theme articulates the circumstances that disposed each reformer to adopt certain strategies of reform. They each discuss how they planned to take political interests into account when implementing certain policy measures, and how they weighed short-term and long-term policies.

The drawing up of the economic programmes followed upon dramatic events that brought about the final decline of the communist era. Once in office, the main objectives of these reformers were to effect an irreversible shift from a command economy to a free market one and to develop market institutions. While the general objective was the same for each reformer, the following pages provide the reader with an account that identifies the factors that induced these reformers to adopt distinct policies and methods for their implementation.

The concrete objectives of each programme were defined in large part by the economic conditions at the time and the economic problems that each reformer identified and addressed. For example, in Poland, Balcerowicz defined the main objectives as dealing with 'the macroeconomic catastrophe and solv[ing] the structural problem of low and declining efficiency'. Poland was suffering from inflation and a shortage of goods, which required, according to Balcerowicz, both radical stabilization measures and long-term structural reforms. Similarly, Bod explains that in Hungary the two main priorities were (1) the transformation of ownership relations, and (2) the maintenance of the functioning of the economy, which at that time meant resolving the country's deficit problem, thereby maintaining its international solvency. This meant that the measures adopted in Hungary were focused on the budget and taxation as well as on privatization measures. Václav Klaus describe the objectives of Czechoslovak reform in terms of a necessity to remove all institutions of central planning and to restore a market economy. His plan had two main strategic objectives: liberalization of prices and foreign trade, and large-scale privatization of state property.

The three reformers also present a range of opinions on the issue of the feasibility of adapting western models in transitional contexts and also on the related issue of western advice and aid. On the one hand, Bod argues that the feasibility of the application of western models and theories to the Hungarian situation depended in large part on political decisions and the existence of the proper institutions to implement them. While foreign advice in these matters is useful, it is however limited, as the foreign advisers' knowledge of the Hungarian economy is not very extensive. On the other hand, both Balcerowicz of Poland and Klaus of Czechoslovakia claim that there is no 'non-standard macroeconomic policy', meaning that the programmes drawn up included standard measures to ensure stability during a structural transition. However, at the same time, Klaus argues that the reform processes in Eastern Europe are unique, and it is up to domestic experts who have a better understanding of the country's situation to implement the reforms: '... foreign economic and legal experts, however good their knowledge of the market system, can hardly give us advice about reform strategy, reform measures and their sequencing'. Balcerowicz, on the other hand, was more open to foreign advice.

The divergence of opinions between Bod, and Klaus and Balcerowicz becomes more apparent in one of the key issues that has defined most discussions of economic policy during the transition: the strategy of implementation and sequencing of reforms, or the 'shock therapy' versus gradualism issue. It is this very complex issue of implementation that defines the second half of this section. While the Polish programme of 1990 and the Czechoslovak programme of 1991 have been generally portrayed as 'shock therapy', 'big bang' programmes, the Hungarian approach is commonly considered to be a more gradual attempt at reform. Balcerowicz of Poland and Klaus of Czechoslovakia emerge from these discussions as having designed the most immediate and comprehensive reforms plans, calling for quick and deep institutional restructuring, accompanied by rapid privatization and full liberalization. Balcerowicz, for example, claims that a reform package that would not be reversible needs to be comprehensive and address all aspects of economic life simultaneously. Furthermore, he argues that this sort of radical change is more effective: 'I sensed that the willingness of the public and of the political elites to accept drastic steps would decline after the first period of "extraordinary politics", that is, the time when the tendency to think and act in terms of a "general good" is strong and sectoral interests are correspondingly weaker ... it was necessary to use this period for a tough economic programme.' Klaus argues that the gradualist approach implies the preservation of the old command economy decision-making institutions. He explains that liberalization of the economy and institutional restructuring must be carried out simultaneously, for 'in this situation it is absolutely necessary to launch a critical mass of reform measures which will rapidly bring about an essential systemic change, to create market conditions in the shortest period of time and at the very beginning and let the market function.' Bod, on the other hand, argues that a plan does not have to induce shock effects to be comprehensive. Bod makes a distinction between the piecemeal reform that defined Hungary during 1968–90 and systemic change, which characterizes the irreversible, long-term changes of the post-1990 reform programmes. Bod argues that the reforms must always be implemented with consideration for the current state of development and the capabilities of existing institutions. According to Bod, if market institutions develop under other than optimal conditions, 'they will operate sub-optimally from the very beginning. The recommendation was therefore to attempt a one-off macroeconomic stabilization and let the new institutions of a market economy evolve afterwards.' The problem, however, is that in the absence of required market institutions it is difficult to secure a lasting one-off stabilization. There is, therefore, a social cost in allowing possible sub-optimal institutions to operate and this cost should be weighed in advance of the implementation of structural reforms.

These differences, among others, played a role in determining the actual sequence in the process of implementing the reforms, and also affected the extent of popular support for the reforms as the effects of the reforms began to be felt.

1. THE GENERAL CONCEPTION OF THE REFORM STRATEGY

Can you please enumerate the two main objectives of the reform process as you perceived them before the process was launched? Can you tell us why these objectives were perceived as the most crucial? Was there any conflict between different members of the reform team regarding the definition of the most important objectives? As the objectives were defined, what were the main policy instruments that were thought of in order to attain these objectives? In other words, did you have, even in general terms, a 'road plan' of how to proceed so as to attain your main objectives?

BALCEROWICZ: To put the Polish economy on the path of efficiency and improve the average standard of living required, first, dealing with the macroeconomic disaster and solving the structural problem of low and declining efficiency.

Macroeconomic stabilization required radical measures: cutting the budget deficit, controlling the money supply and moving towards real positive interest rates. Besides, it was my strong view from the beginning that not only the stabilization but also the asymmetry of the labour market (institutionally strong employees facing non-private and therefore weak employers) required wage controls, hence the strengthening of the so-called *popiwek*, by, for example, progressively taxing the state enterprises' wage increases if they surpassed a certain norm. I was also inclined to think that stabilizing the rate of exchange could provide an important nominal anchor. This presupposed the abolition of the regime of multiple exchange rates and the introduction of internal convertibility for the Polish zloty, which in turn constituted an important change in the economic system. At the same time liberalization of prices was indispensable in order to get rid of massive shortages. There were, therefore, important links between the stabilization and microeconomic liberalization parts of the overall economic programme (price liberalization in turn also constituted an important element of the transformation of the economic system).

The structural problem of low efficiency required a fundamental change in the economic system. With Poland's newly gained freedom to shape her institutions, I believed, we were no longer condemned to search for a kind of 'third way' solution. Instead, we were now able to put into place the least imperfect of the real world economic systems, namely the competitive capitalist market economy. The institutional transformation also included radical changes in the social safety net (for example, introducing mechanisms to deal with open unemployment and strengthening targeted social assistance).

The reasoning here was simple:

(i) first, a market economy is to be preferred to a centrally planned economy;

(ii) second, a private enterprise market economy is to be preferred to 'market socialism', since 'market socialism' has all the main economic weaknesses of the private enterprise market economy (for instance a stronger tendency for unemployment), but less innovativeness and dynamism. Hence I firmly believed that we should rely on 'proven models', which we know of from the real market economies.

Not everything in these economies had proved itself, and

we hoped to avoid the introduction of certain mechanisms which would be difficult to reverse, if not being actually irreversible. My major concern was to avoid adopting a western type of protectionist and overregulated policy with respect to agriculture, especially of the European Community's CAP type, or the sort of industrial policy whereby the state bureaucracy would pick winners by manipulating the tax system or credit policy. State policy with respect to the economy should be as uniform as possible, avoiding detailed interventions. Otherwise a weak public administration would get involved, as in the case of central planning, in widespread bargaining with enterprises about the terms on which they functioned, which would culminate in massive rent seeking and the same type of soft budget constraint for enterprises as in the socialist system.

There was no conflict among the members of the reform team with respect to the most important objectives. There were different views on policy instruments, for example, wage controls or methods of privatization. Some of them were obvious and others were more controversial, at least in the early internal discussions in the narrow group responsible for drawing up the economic programme. The obvious instruments comprised a radical reduction of the budget deficit and of its inflationary financing, and a radical slowing down of the growth of the money supply, involving a shift towards real positive interest rates. The more controversial groups of measures included exchange rate policy and wages policy. There was no disagreement that the system of multiple exchange rates should be abolished and replaced by convertibility at a uniform rate of exchange, but there was some discussion of whether this rate should be flexible or fixed. I opted for the fixed rate in the interests of stabilization.

As far as wages policy is concerned, there were proponents of free wage setting, that is the removal of existing wage controls, for the sake of establishing a market-based wage structure. I was strongly opposed to this view, however. First, because the institutional preconditions for the proper functioning of the labour market were lacking; that is to say, the employee side was strong, owing to the powerful position of the trade unions and the political mobilization of the workers, and the employer side was weak because of the lack of private owners, that is, because of the dominance of the state sector in the economy. Second, as far as I was concerned it was hardly possible that we could successfully stabilize the Polish economy, beset by hyperinflation, while removing such wage controls as already existed.

BOD: The two most important priorities of the programme[1] were the transformation of ownership relations (wide-ranging privatization) and the maintenance of the functioning of the country which, in the case of Hungary in those days, meant first and foremost the safeguarding of our international solvency. The members of the programme drafting team generally accepted that the achievement of the main objectives – reduction of the state share of ownership by way of privatization and the emergence of new businesses; breaking out of the East European economic system and speedy integration with the west; the elimination of subsidies and the winding up of unviable large enterprises – would require sacrifices, the growth of unemployment, and a further rise in prices.

The instruments to attain these goals were to be *macro-economic stabilization and the creation of market institutions*

---

[1]   The programme to which reference is made is the economic manifesto of the (Magyar) Democratic Forum (MDF), the party that later attained a relative majority in Parliament and determined the economic programme of the Government.

and, between the spring of 1989 and the party assembly in October, the economic programme was drawn up in detail, naturally covering the instruments of economic policy as well. Most of the instruments were related to the budget and taxation. The programme included the extension of Value-Added Tax (VAT): at the time, food, services and certain other products given preference by that government were taxed at zero per cent. We also planned *higher energy prices*, partly in order to increase revenues, but much more for reasons of industrial restructuring and to reduce our dependence on Soviet energy. We intended to change the sharing of tax revenues to the benefit of local governments, transferring to them certain welfare and economic functions in the hope that they would be more efficient in collecting taxes than the central authorities.

A similarly detailed chapter addressed the issue of *privatization* and the operation of the remaining public sector. The main elements of the programme were the following: social control of the privatization process, simultaneous application of several privatization techniques, and taking a business approach to the process (meaning sale at realistic prices as the main rule). At the enterprises retained in state ownership for the time being, the programme declared that the form of the so-called 'enterprise council' should be terminated, as it had become the embodiment of the principle of socialist self-government. The establishment of a national property management institution (or holding company), and the decentralization and restructuring of enterprises were also included in our proposal.

KLAUS: When we discussed the reform strategy in our country, in the late 1980s, we all agreed that central planning must be abolished and that the market system must be fully restored. From the very beginning there were, however, two groups of economists with totally different approaches to the reform strategy. The group to which I belonged insisted on rapid removal of all institutions of central planning. Our two main strategic objectives were:

(i) liberalization of prices and of foreign trade; and
(ii) large-scale privatization of state property.

The opposite group argued that first of all the whole economy, and large, state-owned enterprises in particular, should be restructured by means of state assistance and intervention, and only then could the market be introduced. This, in fact, could not have been done without the well-known, long-established practices and institutions of central planning. It proved impossible to reconcile these two approaches and the political conflict between the two groups became unavoidable. Finally, our group succeeded in persuading the parliament, and our reform strategy was accepted by the government and began to be implemented without damaging delay.

Our basic reform plan was based on four main pillars:

(i) liberalization of prices;
(ii) liberalization of foreign trade and introduction of internal current account convertibility;
(iii) very restrictive, anti-inflationary monetary and fiscal policies, and
(iv) privatization.

Price and trade liberalization was necessary in order to force consumers and producers to face real costs, to behave rationally, and to start the process of adaptation to the world economy, based, in principle, on efficient resource allocation. Convertibility of the currency was important for opening our economy and for bringing competition of foreign products to our own markets. But we must admit that price liberalization and currency convertibility were, in fact, steps that were unavoidable. By removing central planning we removed one system of allocation of resources (and of foreign currencies) and we had to put an alternative system of allocation in its place – the price system. Otherwise the economy could not function. We see such a non-system in some other post-communist countries at the present time.

It was equally crucial to maintain a stable currency, given that rational economic behaviour is impossible in an environment of high inflation. That is why we considered slow monetary growth and a balanced government budget to be such important objectives. We have stressed this element more than all other reforming countries. And privatization was necessary so as to put such firms under the control of real owners who would restructure them and force their management to behave rationally. Since we knew from our experience that the state is unable to reshape the productive structure of the enterprises, we were convinced that privatization must be realized prior to the restructuring of existing firms. That is why we adopted a strategy of rapid privatization, supplemented by some non-traditional privatization methods (namely, the voucher scheme).

Regarding the four-pillar plan, it was clear that the four reform steps had to start immediately and in parallel: they complemented one another. They represented the 'hard core' of the whole reform blueprint.

At the time when the reforms were being conceived, did you believe that standard macroeconomic policies applied in market economies could be implemented in your country? Or did you think then that market-oriented policies should be largely adapted to conform to your specific circumstances?

BALCEROWICZ: There was, in my view, no alternative to standard macroeconomic policies, that is to disciplined fiscal and monetary policies, as a means of stopping hyperinflation and of stabilizing the economy. But there were three additional points related to them. First, they had to be supplemented, as already mentioned, by strong wage controls not only in order to break the inflationary momentum, but also because of institutional bias in the labour market in favour of the employees. Second, our enlarged and heterogeneous programme of stabilization had to be linked to the radical liberalization of prices and foreign trade. This was because the task was not only to stop hyperinflation but also to radically remove the shortage economy; otherwise no change in the efficiency of operation of the respective enterprises would have been possible. Third, I was aware that the stabilization and liberalization programme would have to be introduced in an economy that had as yet not fundamentally changed, and thus that it would induce less favourable supply responses than in a largely private economic system. But this, in my view, was no argument against basing our programme on standard macroeconomic policies, since I perceived the alternative strategies to be hopeless or almost hopeless.

BOD: The question of whether we wished to implement the economic programme by applying standard economic policies or instead by adapting to specific Hungarian circumstances can be answered only with the benefit of hindsight. At that time the relevant question was not whether we would achieve macroeconomic stabilization by relying on the usual theories or on the basis of some sort of 'transition economics'. The first question was this: do we want an irreversible break with the state-controlled 'socialist' economy, knowing the immediate losses and political risks ensuing from the transition, or not? The answer was in the affirmative. The second question was whether we should simultaneously undertake both macroeconomic stabilization and the development of market institutions, or did we have to proceed sequentially? The question was debated and the outcome was in favour of simultaneity. It was only after this that we could ask the question of what economic theory would be the basis of macroeconomic stabilization. On the whole, the economic concepts and interrelations applied in advanced market economies directed the thinking of the decision makers. But it was also evident that, without all the necessary institutions in place, a number of unexpected effects could result from time lags and from the measures that were adopted.

KLAUS: Let me first tell you that here is no non-standard macroeconomic policy. An economy in which old institutions of central planning have just been abolished, where quasi-monopolistic market structures are common, and where prices as well as access to hard currencies have just been de-regulated, is very susceptible to inflation and its macroeconomic stability is very fragile. That is why we adopted severe anti-inflationary policies. In contrast with the Polish case, however, wage controls were very lax and played only a marginal role. We put the main stress on restrictive monetary and fiscal policies. In doing that we were not able to prevent an initial jump in prices, but after a few months the rate of inflation stabilized at a reasonably low level, which was the first but very important success of the reform: inflationary expectations were eliminated, and confidence in money was rebuilt. Very soon the positive rate of saving was restored and a transparent economic environment was created.

After the first post-liberalization price increase our central bank was able to ease the monetary restriction somewhat, and we were able to begin applying *standard, non-Keynesian* macroeconomic policies, based on a balanced government budget, stable monetary growth and the principle of neutrality in respect of private sector activities, just as they are applied in most developed market economies.

When thinking about reform policies and measures, how important was it in your mind to introduce irreversible *measures that implied a clear break with the past system and that would make it very difficult to reverse the process? Was this a consideration at all in your thinking, or did you think, instead, that measures should be flexible and allow for reversals if the conditions changed?*

BALCEROWICZ: One of the basic questions I was interested in as a student of economic reforms was, first, why the economic reforms in the socialist countries had been partially or wholly reversed, and second, why they failed to bring about any significant increase in overall efficiency. (As a matter of fact, one of the last papers I published before entering the government was entitled 'On the reformability of the Soviet-type economic system'.) My general response to these questions was that the economic reforms failed because they were not radical enough, that is, they did not quickly pass a certain threshold of necessary changes; or, in other words, a 'critical mass' of such changes was not achieved. So I entered the government with a strong 'anti-gradualist' attitude towards economic reform. This belief was based not only on the experience of the previous reforms but also on the conclusions I drew from social psychology, especially from the theory of cognitive dissonance of Leon Festinger. One of the findings of this theory is that people are more likely to change their attitudes and their behaviour if they are faced with radical changes in their environment that they consider irreversible than if these changes are only gradual.

With respect to the content of the 'critical mass', my view was that a centrally managed economy had a certain 'constructional logic': being a non-market economy it relied on targets, rationing and administrative prices, which in turn require monopolistic and heavily concentrated organizational structures in order to operate this mechanism of coordination. Such structures could be maintained only if organizational rights, that is rights to set up, reorganize and liquidate enterprises, were largely in state hands. According to this view the critical mass should break up the 'constructional logic' of the system by liberalizing prices and foreign trade, removing all the remnants of central allocation of goods and services, breaking up the domestic monopolies and decentralizing the organizational rights – in other words by introducing the freedom of entrepreneurship (liberal property rights).

BOD: As I mentioned in my previous answer, the original economic programme envisaged major and irreversible changes. This should be emphasized once more, for both within the country and in certain international comparisons the view is frequently expressed that the programme of the Hungarian transition was *gradual*, since it did not undertake the so-called shock therapy. Here it is necessary to clarify a few points. In Hungary, economic programmes of various parties competed against one another. In the course of the contest radical voices dominated at first. The parties that did not reckon on government responsibility could more easily compile consistent programmes, in which they did not mention the inevitable costs of implementing the transition, nor the necessary compromises with ideals. A party with a high chance of sharing governmental responsibility, such as the MDF, had to be more careful in its formulations and had to answer practical questions as well. The more mature a programme is, the less radical it appears: the radicalism of a practical programme will, of necessity, lag behind verbal radicalism.

Another reason why the Hungarian government's programme was described outside the country – without good reason – as too cautious was that initial deregulatory measures had been implemented by previous administrations. In other countries, such measures became the task of the new governments. Just take prices as an example. Since the previous government had already abolished official price controls over 70 per cent of the products, the new economic programme could not do more than address the scheduling and content of the remaining 20–25 per cent. It was natural that countries entering the transition with more centralized economies could promise to extend the range of freely priced goods from 10 to 70 per cent in a single step. In the case of Hungary, such a degree of further deregulation was no longer possible. Fortunately, the government did not enter the unwarranted 'competition in radicalism'.

KLAUS: From the very beginning we were very suspicious about the old institutions of the centrally planned system. We knew that to initiate real reform it was necessary to break through the wall of these institutions, to destroy them, otherwise they would always slow down the reform process and hinder the emergence of the new market institutions. In this sense, the reforms should be irreversible. Our reform achievements should definitely prevent the re-emergence of institutions of the previous system, but for this to happen a necessary precondition is, of course, macroeconomic stability. The essence of our reform was not to design a precise plan and detailed timetable for the process of economic transformation towards the market system; rather, we wanted to remove the obstacles to a spontaneous process of evolution of markets and private property. The four basic pillars of our reform – its hard core – are irreversible, but economic legislation and standard government economic policies in our country are as flexible as they are in developed market economies: it is a process of learning by doing.

As policy measures were being devised, how did you assess your ability to implement them? What were the main factors, in your view, affecting the capacity for implementation? Were you optimistic about the administrative competence of the system? What was your assessment of the chances of assembling a minimum core of bureaucracy that could carry out the policy measures in an environment that lacked familiarity with the instruments that were to be used? What were the first steps that you took in organizing a new government structure?

BALCEROWICZ: I was aware of the administrative difficulties. I knew that the state economic administration was rather weak in terms of both numbers and competence. But I also realized that it was not possible to change it quickly for the better because of the shortage of people with a good knowledge of the market economy and because of the great number of urgent problems. So basically it was with this weak administration that I had to work. In this situation I did two things. First, within two or three weeks I formed a group of my closest associates, consisting partly of newcomers and partly of insiders, some of whom I already knew. This required that I quickly dismiss some people from their functions in order to make room for the newcomers.

With respect to the members of the newly formed economic team, I tried to create a relationship of trust and a sense of a common mission. Something of the *esprit de corps* had truly emerged and was an important factor in keeping the group and the programme together.

Second, I made structural changes to the institutions of which I was in charge. In the Ministry of Finance we abolished the bloated Department of Prices (responsible mainly for price controls), and we created, practically form scratch, the departments dealing with financial institutions (banks and insurance companies), which were headed by a colleague of mine, Stefan Kowalec. We also strengthened the departments responsible for the budget. In my office of Deputy Prime Minister I created a number of coordinating committees and a group of strategic advisers distinct from those who were dealing with current problems. A very important role was played by the section which was responsible for overall coordination and for dealing with the political aspects of the economic programme, that is, with the political parties, parliament, the office of the president, the trade unions, the mass media, and so on. This section was very ably managed by Jerzy Kozminski.

BOD: The difficulties in implementing the government programme began with surveying the state of the state administration. In the spring and summer of 1990, the Hungarian state administration stood practically idle. Some of the government departments, in their existing form, became superfluous: the National Planning Office or the National Materials and Prices Office, for instance. A large number of the senior staff left. This was in part motivated by the better-paying jobs offered by the mushrooming domestic and foreign businesses. The joint ventures and joint banks were particularly willing to recruit former government and party officials at a time when it had not yet become clear that the opposition to the communist party would gain a sweeping victory.

Another factor that promoted the redundancy of state administration was that in previous decades there had been no clear-cut separation of state administration and the party bureaucracy. It is well known that state institutions had their counterparts within the party. The party instructor used to take part in the managerial meetings of the ministries, and the more important matters had been decided by the staff of the Central Committee. The decision-making procedure had reckoned with the existence of the party apparatus not merely on an informal basis. At the Planning Office, for instance, there had been a well-regulated procedure for preparing economic policy documents: the assignment came from the Central Committee, the draft was prepared by the staff of the state administration and went successively higher up as far as the Economic Committee (officially, a government body), and then the Economic Policy Committee of the party (officially a party body, with much overlapping in membership) made the decision; then the document was returned to the state administration for fine-tuning and implementation.

Another characteristic example is my experience with the Institute for Public Opinion Polls, which in the second half of the 1980s belonged to the government. For research into enterprise behaviour, we needed certain polls (on such matters as expectations of inflation, consumer and employee habits). Being head of the department I felt myself of sufficient rank to ring the director of the institute, a well-known expert on communications and a TV personality. He said that the 'agitation and propaganda' department of the party had the right of decision over the operations and products of the institute; I should turn to them for a permission. Well, I did not.

The rapid collapse of the establishment party put an end to all this. The new political forces faced a grave dilemma. If they kept the state administration as it was, with the inherited structure and staff, they would have a better chance of re-starting the operation of government. In that case, the new structures would have to be created and the old ones terminated as they went along. The other possible solution was to start out with the desired structure right away, undertaking the extra burden of a major reorganization.

The preparation of a work plan concerning the government structure had been in progress previously. The plan envisaged fewer, but more fully integrated, traditional ministries, and a number of new government agencies that were required for the new functions. I must admit that this relatively well-elaborated section of the programme had little influence on decision making. Eventually, though, some of its ideas were implemented, such as the merger of the Ministries for Industry and Trade or the establishment of the ministry responsible for infrastructure.

The reorganization and relaunching of the state administration took a good six months. I experienced this period already as Minister for Industry and Trade. The ministers and their staffs, with tremendous effort, established the new structure by the second half of 1990; this, of course, took a very great deal of energy and much time. The public, naturally, knew little about the transformation of state administration – the basic tenor of the press was that 'A hundred days are gone; nothing has been accomplished yet'. From the distance of two or three years I now tend to accept that this was the right way. It is certain that this new framework enabled me to reduce the number of staff drastically. Whereas, for instance, more than 200 people used to deal with domestic trade, I assigned only 60 to this function within the new structure - and the new staff was sufficient to deal with the changing tasks of the state.

KLAUS: I have always been pessimistic about the capabilities of state bureaucrats to implement reforms. That is why we designed our reform programme to be based on a very limited number of reform measures organized by the government. This is especially true as regards privatization: we rejected the idea that privatization should be mostly or exclusively based on traditional textbook methods (that would require the restructuring of firms, complicated evaluation of their assets, dealing with their debts, cleaning up their balance sheets, and so forth). That is why we made use of a voucher method that was quick and simple enough in distributing state property among individuals. We were warned by external experts and advisers about taking this course but we were right to disregard their advice and to follow our own views and priorities. We were not so much afraid of using non-traditional, non-standard instruments (even though they were not tested by previous experience), provided they conformed to the market process. What we were afraid of, however, were the ambitions of state bureaucrats to control markets and to choose the future owners of state property, as is now being done - with very bad results - in many post-communist countries.

What role, if any, was played by foreign advisers *in influencing your thinking about economic reform? Did you actively seek external advice at that point?*

BALCEROWICZ: As I was interested in the problems of economic transformation and stabilization long before I entered the government, that was when I developed the main ideas: radical stabilization and liberalization to deal with the macroeconomic problem of hyperinflation and massive shortages, unification of the exchange rate and the introduction of convertibility, the shift from import substitution to outward-looking growth, rapid privatization and other fundamental institutional reforms, and so on. In this respect foreign advisers played an important role in strengthening my own beliefs. This was especially true of the idea of radical stabilization and liberalization, which was discussed and supported by the specially created Economic Council in December 1989. It had such prominent foreign members as Michael Bruno, Stanley Fisher, Stanislaw Gomulka, Tadeusz Rybczynski, Jeffrey Sachs and Stanislaw Wellisz. Jeffrey Sachs, David Lipton, Stanislaw Gomulka and Jacek Rostowski also helped with the elaboration of the general programme on other occasions. This was also true of Polish advisers and associates such as Marek Dabrowski, Stefan Kawalec and Karol Lutkowski.

Some foreign advisers were also putting forward specific proposals. For example, Stanislaw Gomulka and Jeffrey Sachs independently proposed setting up some privatization funds as intermediaries in the massive privatization of state enterprises. Jeff Sachs had also put forward the idea of a stabilization fund to support the introduction of convertibility of the Polish zloty. Jacek Rostowski worked out the concept of special financial institutions, which would offer conditional financial assistance to state enterprises turned down by the normal commercial banks.

BOD: At first I had a fairly mixed opinion of the activity of foreign consultants in the International Monetary Fund and the World Bank. In their capacity as creditors, they have good reason to form an accurate picture of the country and to give sound advice. At the time of the change in our political systems, these institutions had more than eight years of experience of Hungary. A good number of their staff members had been involved in the region for a long time: their advice and warnings were well worth listening to. These organizations are criticized from time to time because, it is said, they give schoolbook recipes for countries in different circumstances. There may be some truth in this, but one should also admit that decision makers in all countries tend to believe that their problems are unique, although in most cases these are well-known, recurrent economic difficulties.

The advice of the international organizations on matters of macroeconomics is very useful; but the main role must belong to the experts of the country concerned when it comes to the setting up of economic institutions. I remember very well the mid-1980s, when the transformation of state enterprises into self-governing organizations was one of the Hungarian reform ideas. This type of reform, which turned out to be very detrimental to further development, was praised as progress by the international organizations as well. On the whole, it can be stated that the consultants of these organizations have also learnt a great deal from the transformation of Central and Eastern Europe.

We gained little of value from those who came from academic circles. Most of them, naturally, have little or no knowledge of the country or of its state administration. As a former researcher, perhaps I may allow myself the remark that some of them would have welcomed the newly emerging market economies if they had developed in accordance with their own hypotheses. However, this type of consultant acquired some importance because, as regular interviewees and authors, they influenced western public opinion at a time when there was scant information on the new movements and governments.

Since the change in regime, many useful and valuable Hungarians have returned to the country. True, some came with somewhat dubious proposals, but this, too, characterized more the reform communist era and the interregnum. Several of them have since given up their consulting work for positions in government or in the business community. Since they have a satisfactory knowledge of the country but have spent their formative years in the environment of a market economy, they can be truly useful.

KLAUS: The reform process in each of the former socialist countries is unique; there is no past experience of it. Therefore foreign economic and legal experts, however good their knowledge of the market system, can hardly give us much advice about reform strategy, reform measures and their sequencing. In this respect I always preferred listening to our domestic economists as they knew better the real situation in our country. Foreign experts could give us good advice on how to develop market institutions and instruments, rather than how to sequence and time our reform policies or how to privatize our enterprises.

Was the experience of other countries that reformed or stabilized their economies considered or regarded as applicable? Did you study their experiences or try to get advice from those who were familiar with those episodes? Did your learning from other experiences relate mainly to the positive or the negative aspects or consequences of the reforms?

BALCEROWICZ: For many years I had been intererested in the economic reforms in what were then socialist countries. As I have said before, my main conclusion from these studies was that they failed because they were not radical enough. This also applied in the relatively most comprehensive but gradual reform in Hungary. To my mind this negative experience strongly called for a radical approach.

I was also familiar with the main examples of reforms in the non-socialist countries. Indeed, one of my main interests in the 1980s concerned economic transformations that brought about unexpectedly good results. As I mentioned, I spent five months in 1985 as a visiting fellow at the Institute of Development Studies at the University of Sussex in England, investigating the South Korean case, and to some extent the Taiwanese economy. In the autumn of 1988 I spent three months in Marburg in West Germany studying the Experience of Ludwig Erhard's reforms in 1948. I was also interested in the stabilization programmes in Latin America. My general impression was that the applicability of these experiences to the Polish case was rather limited, because the initial situation in Poland was much more difficult given the burden of the previous system, and the scope of the necessary changes was much bigger. Still, there were some lessons.

With respect to stabilization, I knew that, irrespective of the institutional differences, hyperinflation required a radical approach in order to break the inflationary momentum. The institutional differences had, to my mind, two consequences. First, given the asymmetry of the labour market, related to the absence of private owners in what was still a socialist economy, there was a strong need for tough wage controls going beyond the macroeconomic rationale for such controls in terms of breaking the inflationary inertia. Second, because the tough programme of stabilization had to be introduced in a basically non-private economy, its supply response was more uncertain and could be worse than in an economy even of the Latin American type. But the alternative strategies had, to my mind, much less of a chance for success.

With respect to the elimination of shortages, which constituted one of the basic short-run goals of the programme,
the problem was price controls and the rigidity of supply,
and not the 'soft budget constraint' of enterprises. The latter, in
my opinion, was one of the main factors responsible for their
low efficiency, as it implied the absence of competition. I
remembered that in Yugoslavia and in many parts of the
Indian economy there prevailed a 'soft budget constraint'
with no shortages. On the other hand, price controls were
strongly associated with shortages in some Latin American
countries, for example Brazil in the 1980s, not to mention
the war economy in western countries or the socialist economies.

Another important lesson was that, in the absence of competition, import substitution and the heavy regulation of the
economy are sufficient to cause low efficiency and widespread rent-seeking; private property cannot remedy this
situation. These were the negative conclusions I drew from
the experiences of the many Latin American countries and
India, and from the economic literature, especially from the
writings of Bella Balassa and Anne Krueger.

BOD: It is evident that countries facing similar historic
tasks should learn from one another's successes and mistakes. Nevertheless, I could not say that the countries of the
former Soviet empire should have paid much attention to
one another. External coercion had forced peoples of different natures and different cultures into the Soviet sphere of
interest and, in spite of the similarities, the ways and means
of making the break have also been different.

Before the free elections, I visited Estonia and Poland.
Estonia was still awaiting the elections, while Poland had
been in the thick of political transformation for many years.
Yet it would have been difficult to learn anything in the

positive sense from the Polish example, as the power relations in the Polish parliament were the results of negotiations, whereas Hungary was preparing for free elections, in which there was no negotiated place for the successor party of the communists. The countries at a more or less similar stage of economic advancement (Czechoslovakia, Hungary and Poland) stood at different levels of liberalization and openness in trade, hence the agenda of economic transformation had also to be different.

For me, the most interesting visit was the first one that I paid to the former GDR in the autumn of 1990. As Minister for Industry and Trade, I went mainly to promote the case of the Hungarian enterprises that were losing their markets there. But seeing the impact of genuine shock therapy was extraordinarily useful for me as an economic policy maker. This visit confirmed my view that ways must be sought to allow for an organic development and that the necessary shocks affecting the economy both internally and externally should not be regarded as an occasion to 'clear the table'.

KLAUS: Of course we followed the experiences of some other countries that reformed their economies in parallel with our own, especially those of Hungary and Poland, but I must say that what we learned from them was mainly on the negative side. Hungarian economic reform under Kádár's communist regime was a typical 'third way' reform that could only destabilize the economy without bringing important results in transforming it to a market system. The post-Kádár developments still need to be analysed and appreciated. And Poland had not yet fully succeeded in achieving macroeconomic stability without which no economic reform – that is, institutional changes – can be successful. Trade unions too strong and the existence of too many political parties complicate the reform and economic policy dramatically. We learned from the experience of these countries that economic reform measures must be systemic, consistent and quick, that social consent is indispensable, and that the reform process must be led by a strong right-wing political party that has the support of the majority of citizens.

2. ON THE PARTICULAR TYPES OF REFORM MEASURES ADOPTED

What were the main elements you considered necessary for a reform programme to be successful? Please discuss your personal perspective on the relative importance, sequencing, and correlation of the various reform measures that comprised your programmes.

BALCEROWICZ: In my view, there were several necessary conditions for establishing a competitive and efficient economy.

(i) An economy predominantly in private hands.
(ii) A sufficient degree of competition.
(iii) An economy outwardly and not inwardly oriented: one of the main lessons I drew from my studies at the Foreign Trade Section of the Warsaw School of Economics was that the strategy of import substitution is bound to fail. An outward-looking strategy presupposed, among other things, currency convertibility within a tough macroeconomic strategy in order to contain the growth of domestic costs. An export-oriented strategy and competition also required a liberal foreign trade regime, and above all the elimination of the quantitative restrictions and the granting of universal access to foreign trade.

(iv) Stable money: I was fully aware of the harm hyper-inflation causes to growth. Stability required among other things the institutional independence of the central bank. A law establishing this independence was in the first package of laws presented by the government and passed by the Polish Sejm [parliament] at the end of 1989.

(v) An important but limited role for the State: I knew of private sectors over-protected and over-regulated and, hence, highly inefficient – for example, in India and much of Latin America. These practices were clearly to be avoided. I had a vision of the set of functions that constituted the natural sphere of the state's competence, that is, in which no other agency could replace the state. These were as follows:

- stabilizing and maintaining the macro-stability of the economy;
- the supply of public goods;
- carrying out foreign economic policy (largely trade liberalization);
- foreign debt negotiations;
- providing a social safety net, necessary in order to face the consequences of dismantling price subsidies, and the side effects of the new economic order (above all, unemployment) without overburdening the economy.

I had a clear perception from the very beginning that because of the inherited hyperinflation we had to choose between an almost hopeless strategy and a risky strategy. There was no option without risk. An almost hopeless strategy would have consisted in neglecting the stabilization part of the programme, and in focusing instead on the transformation part, especially on privatization.

It was and it is still my view that the strategy of tolerating hyperinflation would make stabilization more and more difficult with the passage of time, and the related chaos of hyperinflation would make rapid transformation, including privatization, scarcely possible. So this strategy, 'privatization first, stabilization later', would most likely have resulted in neither privatization nor stabilization.

It was thus reasonable to choose a strategy that was merely risky, but not hopeless: that of starting stabilization and transformation at about the same time. Stabilization measures and the liberalization part of the programme of transformation could be introduced more rapidly than privatization and other deep institutional reforms. The radical strategy consisted, therefore, in the rapid introduction of the interrelated stabilization and liberalization package while at the same time undertaking more time-consuming institutional reforms. This implied, given the differences in the possible speed, that radical stabilization and liberalization had to be introduced in the economy while it was not yet fundamentally transformed. The risk of this strategy was that the supply response of such an economy was smaller and could be more uncertain than in private economies. But I always compared these risks with those of delaying stabilization or liberalization (or implementing them gradually). It was obvious to me that the latter strategies are hopeless or almost hopeless.

I viewed the economic reform in terms of a radical and comprehensive package, the elements of which complement one another. So the question about relative importance is not easy to answer. Within the overall process of economic transformation, I distinguished between liberalization and deep institutional changes. I knew that the former can be implemented more rapidly than the latter. At the same time, slowing down liberalization and stabilization, in order to enable them to keep pace with the fundamental institutional reform, was for me a more hazardous option than trying to implement all the changes with maximum speed, knowing, however, that stabilization and liberalization had to be largely completed before the institutional framework of the economy could be radically changed.

Within liberalization, the freeing of prices was a crucial measure, necessary for the rapid elimination of shortages and for obtaining better price information. Radical price liberalization required, in my view, a decisive liberalization of foreign trade, which in turn included the unification of exchange rates and currency convertibility. They were also indispensable for obtaining better relative prices. In addition, the fixing of the newly unified exchange rate played an important role in the programme of stabilization, and the introduction of convertibility signalled a decisive break with the past partial and unsuccessful reforms.

Liberalization also included the elimination of the restrictions on the creation and growth of private firms. This was a very important part of a legal framework for economic activity, as it introduced the mechanism of free entry and enabled the spontaneous growth of the private sector. Generally speaking, I perceived the legal framework of the economy as a set of general laws, which determine among other things the types and composition of concrete institutions, for instance, enterprises, tax offices, budgetary units, financial intermediaries, and so on.

As far as these institutions are concerned, the privatization of enterprises was for me the key part of the institutional restructuring. I viewed privatization as the most important type of enterprise reform, and as the most important condition for enterprise restructuring. The extension of private enterprise was, to my mind, crucial for solving the main structural problem of the Polish economy (and of all the post-socialist economies, for that matter): that of low and falling efficiency. But I remembered that the potential inherent in the private sector can be fully released only if there is competition and an outward orientation of the economy. This is why a *liberal foreign trade regime* was for me an important complement to privatization and an important condition for increasing the overall efficiency of the economy. I also believed that some increase in that efficiency might be achieved through foreign trade liberalization, free prices and hardening of the enterprises' budget constraint, preceding the full privatization of state enterprises. However, in order to obtain the maximum possible increase in efficiency, privatization and other changes must be combined.

I viewed *wage determination* as connected to the ownership structure of the economy, that is, to its privatization. The absence of private owners gives rise to an institutional imbalance within the labour market, and hence to wage-push. The intensity of this tendency depended, in my view, on the inherited macroeconomic situation, and on the role and militancy of the trade unions. Both of these factors made wage-push in Poland stronger than in Czechoslovakia and Hungary, and in my view it called for stronger wage controls. An additional reason for these controls was, of course, the inherited hyperinflation. But I was fully aware that any wage controls are imperfect mechanisms for slowing down wage pressure generated by strong socio-institutional forces, and that these controls bring about some microeconomic distortions; besides, the efficiency of wage controls declines over time.

All this strengthened, to my mind, the case for rapid privatization as the only way to remove the institutional imbalance that was generating the excessive wage pressure. But I also knew that the mechanisms of wage determination differ even in capitalistic economies, depending on the structure and the role of the trade unions and on the related properties of the collective bargaining process. This was one of the points I saw as crucial in the Polish situation. Given the 'trade-unionist' tradition of the opposition movement 'Solidarity', which brought down socialism in Poland, this was a very sensitive point, and I delayed its resolution to the latter part of the economic programme, when it was hoped that there would be many more private employers. But I supported the development of employers' organizations and that of the consumers' movement as countervailing forces to the trade unions.

I considered *strengthening the independence of the central bank* to be a key to stable monetary policy. A law to this effect was enacted as early as the autumn of 1989. The reform of the commercial banks played a crucial role in the general economic reform, and it included setting up new, largely private banks, and strengthening the capabilities of the existing state commercial banks, inter alia by organizing the twinning arrangements between them and their western counterparts.

The tax reform also figured largely in the transformation programme. One of the main directions here was the elimination of the very widespread tax breaks and concessions, which were often granted on an ad hoc basis. I considered this a necessary condition for the hardening of enterprise 'budget constraints', and the emergence of the market. In addition, tax reform comprised the introduction of Value-Added Tax and of a comprehensive system of personal income tax.

Budgetary reforms included first of all, the elimination of some fifty extra-budgetary funds so as to increase the transparency and completeness of the budgetary process. The introduction of genuine local government also required many important changes in public finance. Another important element was health service reform.

From the very beginning I considered the creation of a social safety net to be a necessary complement to radical market-oriented reform, which entailed, among other things, slashing the price subsidies on basic goods. At the same time I was very much afraid of 'over-socializing' the early phase of the transition, that is, of burdening the economy with social overheads of such magnitude that they would stifle economic development.

Income distribution was not one of my overriding concerns. I considered the transformation of the economic system as a way to generate lasting development for all – much more important than trying to keep income differentials within some predetermined range. My belief has been that what matters here is not only the absolute magnitude but, much more, how closely the differentials are linked to economic performance. In the previous politico-economic system, the income differentials were, contrary to widespread belief, pretty wide and at the same time only loosely linked to economic performance. What mattered was the monopolistic position and the role in the political–bureaucratic hierarchy. The transition to a competitive market economy could, in my view, increase the income differentials but at the same time also strengthen their link with economic performance. Besides, in economies with free entry and exit, income differentials are less pronounced and lasting than in the heavily regulated monopolistic economy with a large extent of rent-seeking. I believed, therefore, that some of the conditions conducive to high efficiency are also important for keeping income differentials in check and for strengthening their link with economic performance.

International organizations played an important supplementary role in my view. The role of the IMF consisted, above all, in giving credibility to our economic programme. This was especially important in the Polish case, as the negotiations with our foreign debtors and also the official assistance form western governments depended on the IMF's stamp of approval. Besides, I valued the technical advice from the IMF, especially with respect to the tax system. I viewed the World Bank, and later the European Bank for Reconstruction and Development (EBRD), as important potential sources of capital, especially with regard to infrastructure (such as railways, or the energy sector) and important institutional reforms (including enterprise and financial sector restructuring). I regarded these sources of capital as particularly important in the first period of reform, in which one could not (owing to the inherent uncertainty) count on a greater inflow of foreign private investment.

I considered foreign aid in general as secondary to the opening of the western markets. But some forms of foreign assistance were, in my view, important. This applied, above all, to those mechanisms that could speed up the transformation of some important institutional segments of the economy by the increased transfer of specialized know-how or by creating some new institutions in Poland, such as the 'twinning arrangements' between the Polish state commercial banks and western partners, or setting up the business advisory service to help the potential or existing small entrepreneurs to draw up business plans. I also strongly supported the creation of new foreign sources of capital for the private sector in Poland, for instance, the Polish American Enterprise Fund. The billion-dollar stabilization fund, consisting of contributions from the western governments, was for me an important factor in introducing the convertibility of the Polish zloty.

BOD: The recurrent mistake of the hesitant, stop–go economic policy experiments of the 1970s and 1980s in Hungary was that they contained too many, and frequently contradictory, objectives. The ritual party congresses, organized every five years, and the published national economic plans, had a particular attraction for political fantasy. From all this, Hungarian economists did draw the conclusion that a successful economic policy can have one, or at most two or three, major objectives. However, at the heart of the transition is the fact that almost every element of the system will have to change almost at the same time. In view of the constraints of administrative capabilities, one or two tasks can be deliberately postponed, but two different systems of economic logic cannot function within a single system for very long. (This is why the Hungarian NEM could not be ultimately successful, for its internal economic logic increasingly differed from the essentially unreformed logic of domestic politics or of international relations.)

In comparison with the other countries of the region, there was relatively less to be done in the area of deregulation liberalization of wages, further deregulation of price controls and foreign trade, additional steps towards the convertibility of the currency), as good progress had been made in all these areas previously.

Therefore, I would place the setting up of the new economic institutions and the legal framework at the top of the agenda: the setting up of the Anti-Monopoly Office, a law on the privatization of shops, compensation laws, clarification of the legal status of the privatization agency, a new accounting law, a banking law, a law to establish an autonomous central bank, the regulation of unemployment benefits by law, setting up regional retraining and assistance institutions, a law on concessions, a bankruptcy law, and so on. I should mention here that, although I ranked this first in importance, the enacting of these laws took nearly three years, even with strenuous efforts; and, according to all signs, the task of institutional development will remain with us for many years to come.

The reform of the budget and of taxation was also a

significant task of the new parliament. Since the ownership role of the state has been reduced with privatization, economic policy can be conducted largely through the budget. The parliament enacted a number of laws and amendments affecting revenues; however, the procedures for the preparation and endorsement of the budget are still being developed.

Privatization deserves special emphasis: it has a bearing on the development of institutions and its importance is truly far-reaching. The mode and technique of privatization constitute a hard choice that determines economic structures and even social relations. The Hungarian strategy, in contrast to restitution, to distribution and to other procedures that accord preference to those already within the system, is the one most in conformity with the market, the most liberal. Its essence is the sale of state assets, basically without government-initiated financial turn-around, and without corporate restructuring.

One motivating force in choosing such a privatization strategy was the inherited external and internal indebtedness of the Hungarian state. If the assets are not distributed on the basis of citizens' rights, and they are not granted to the employees and managers who happen to work at the given firm but are rather sold for cash, then the majority of the buyers will be foreigners. And so it turned out: until now, more than three-quarters of the proceeds of privatization have been realized in convertible currencies. The foreign exchange income obtained in this way contributed significantly towards eliminating, by the middle of 1991, foreign indebtedness as the main concern of economic policy.

The other reason for adopting this strategy was more political in nature. Before and immediately after the elections, the so-called liberal parties supported privatization as fast as possible and with as few regulations as possible, partly because of their economic approach, partly because they did not get into the new government and they distrusted the government's privatization activities. As Minister for Industry and Trade, I frequently had the experience that they treated my ideas concerning the preliminary break-up or improvement of the enterprise as if they had been meant only to cover up for delaying privatization. Given this political pressure, the ruling parties and the government tried hard to take the sting out of this criticism. But another peculiar political circumstance also supported the strengthening of the market-based privatization philosophy that objectively gives an advantage to foreign buyers: in our conditions the only alternative would be management buy-out, whereby the old *nomenklatura* or the profiteers (or both) became rich. It should be remembered that the process of privatization was launched during the term of the last reform communist government without the effective legal and institutional protection of the public interest. The vast majority of the cases of initial privatization carried out by the previous government ranged from the justly objectionable to the downright outrageous. Had the interregnum continued longer, the evolution of the 'capitalism of cronies' – the 'privatization by looting' – would have been stopped by public outrage. The democratic government channelled the process, whereby it enjoyed acceptance by and the support of society. It seems as though the Hungarian employee has hitherto been more willing to accept that Mr Smith might acquire his company and, with a high degree of probability, might make him redundant, than to accept that Mr Kovacs (*alias* Comrade Kovacs) might do the same to him.

KLAUS: The question of choosing the optimal reform package and identifying the appropriate sequencing of the reform is a favourite topic of many confused theoreticians in the discussions about economic transformation, and the literature in this field is becoming enormous. My practical experience, however, tells me that the problem is very often misunderstood.

What is important for the reform to be successful is a clear vision of where to go, a pragmatic reform strategy, and the courage to begin. After forty years of social engineering and devastating communist experiments, it was clear to us that the only system that can ensure long-term prosperity for our country is a normally functioning market economy based on private property and private initiative. When discussing the optimal reform package for a radical transformation it is important to realize that democracy, freedom and market economy cannot be 'introduced', they cannot be implanted into an unprepared or uncooperative society from outside, and cannot be realized as a single act. The transformation of a whole system is a prolonged process with millions of participating actors – human beings – who play their independent and sometimes conflicting roles. It is a process based on the constructive evolution of new institutions and of different modes of human conduct accompanying them. It is mostly a spontaneous process which cannot – without destroying its substance and inner logic – be planned, organized, constructed or master-minded by enlightened intellectuals, scientists or academics, or by ambitious and election-minded politicians.

One has to understand that the abolition of central planning and communist party control over the economy creates a very dangerous situation. The government loses its traditional tools of economic policy in a situation where the whole economy is still state-owned. Uncontrolled and irresponsible management of state-owned enterprises can in a very short time create huge disequilibria and bring the economy close to total collapse. The results of *perestroika* in the former USSR are self-evident in this respect.

It became clear that in this situation it is absolutely necessary to launch a critical mass of reform measures which will rapidly bring about an essential systemic change: to create in the shortest period of time, and at the very beginning, elementary market conditions and then let the market function. In short, we must liberalize, deregulate and privatize, even if by doing that we are confronted with rather weak and therefore not fully efficient markets.

It is also important to keep in mind that the reform is not a theoretical issue. It takes place in real conditions, it affects real and vital interests of particular groups and strata of the population, and those interests are reflected in politics. It means that attempts to follow a master-minded ideal blueprint of reform are simply not feasible in the real world. The reformers must push the reform measures on all fronts and try to have them in place as quickly as possible, otherwise hesitation and delay can result in political obstacles and significant departure from the goal of the reform.

Bearing all this in mind it is obvious that in order to make markets function it is necessary to liberalize the economy. We inherited a fossil structure of distorted prices of goods and services, multiple exchange rates, and an economy isolated from the world by the state monopoly of foreign trade. So, the relatively easy part of the reform package to get started was the liberalization of markets. Liberalization of prices and foreign trade and the introduction of so-called internal convertibility of the currency, allowing for free access to hard currencies for economic agents, can be accomplished overnight. But two conditions are indispensable for them to produce successful results: first, restrictive financial policy is a primary tool with which the government can attempt to minimize inflation; second, currency convertibility and exchange rate unification must be supported by a comfortable level of foreign reserves, so stand-by loans from the IMF and other international financial institutions at the very beginning of the liberalization are of crucial importance for stabilization of the exchange rate and for anchoring prices.

Other elements of the reform package, such as privatization, institution building and re-designing the legal framework, are of a long-term nature and they will be carried out through the whole transformation period. It is necessary, however, to launch these processes at the very beginning of the reform. Clarification of ownership rights and the creation of private business are a precondition for microeconomic adjustment which can only bring about substantial change in the performance of the economy. Privatization must therefore be rapid and massive and must affect both small business outlets and large state-owned industries. The first of these tasks were covered in our country by so-called small privatization, under which small businesses are privatized either through public auctions or through restitution to previous owners. The privatization of large enterprises, however, cannot be accomplished by traditional methods alone. Bearing in mind the huge extent of state property, the level of domestic savings and the time constraint, we had to invent and are now implementing non-traditional methods of voucher privatization enabling rapid distribution of property among the participating population. In our approach, privatization is a method of enterprise restructuring which only the profound interests of the owners, and not government bureaucracy, can effectively accomplish.

Institution building involves establishing dozens of new institutions ranging from the restructuring of the government itself and establishing a two-tier banking system to founding a stock market and tax offices capable of administering the new tax system. Together with the new legal system, they require continuous improvements. The reform also has its social dimension and our constant effort is to make it socially sustainable. The egalitarian income distribution under socialism and social quasi-security was devastating for labour, morale and working habits, and it destroyed entrepreneurial initiative. These elements must therefore be eliminated and replaced by a targeted social safety net supporting those in real need. In the liberalization phase, characterized by risks of high inflation, it was important for us also to maintain within the framework of restrictive macroeconomic policies some degree of wage controls, which contributed significantly to rapid deceleration of the inflation rate.

All these components of the reform package must be tackled simultaneously and only their joint implementation can bring about the necessary systemic change.

How far did the issue of 'shock therapy' versus 'gradualism' play a role in your perception of the reform?

BALCEROWICZ: I never used the expression 'shock therapy' in my public statements, as this is an emotional term often used by the proponents of gradualism against the alternative approach. It is the concentrated introduction of a number of radical measures. As I have already partly explained, I supported a radical approach for a number of general reasons. First, gradual measures are likely to be reversible since they do not overcome the inertia of the previous economic system. Second, people are more likely to accept the inevitability of acting in new ways when they are confronted with radical changes in their situation than when they face incremental changes. This was one of the main lessons I remembered from my studies of social psychology. Third, I sensed that the willingness of the public and of the political elites to accept drastic steps would decline after the first period of 'extraordinary politics' – the time when the tendency to think and act in terms of a 'general good' is strong and sectional interests are correspondingly weaker. Therefore, it was important to use this period for a tough economic programme.

There were also some more specific arguments in favour of a radical approach both for stabilization and for liberalization. Inherited hyperinflation clearly called for a tough stabilization programme in order to break the inflationary dynamic. A gradualist anti-inflationary programme would have been, to my mind, rather like trying to put out a great fire slowly. It would have meant tolerating hyperinflation for a longer time, and as a result the costs of eliminating it could have been higher and the risk of failure could have been greater. Besides, it seemed highly doubtful whether in the conditions of macroeconomic chaos it would have been possible to implement a meaningful institutional change.

There were also some important arguments in favour of radical liberalization. Radical removal of restrictions in respect of private activity was an obvious measure. It had largely been done by late 1988 by the government of Mieczyslaw Rakowski. As far as the liberalization of prices was concerned, a gradual approach would not have been able to eliminate shortages quickly, and this was important not only for the consumers but also for the efficient operation of enterprises and in order to boost their propensity to innovate. Besides, under the gradual approach to price liberalization, the quality of the price information would improve only slowly and this would have meant a correspondingly low quality of information in the enterprises' financial results. It would have been very difficult, therefore, to harden their budget constraint, and the decisions of the autonomous enterprises were bound to be of a low quality too. The administration of prices inherent in the gradualist approach would have absorbed the scarce administrative resources of the government, which in any case faced an unusual number of unprecedented problems.

Radical price liberalization was therefore for me an obvious element of the total package. But this, in turn, called for radical liberalization of foreign trade, embracing the introduction of the convertibility of the Polish zloty, the removal of quantitative restrictions, freedom to engage in foreign trade, and so forth. Otherwise it would have been impossible to ensure a proper check on the domestic producers who enjoyed dominant positions on the home market. Besides, I perceived foreign trade liberalization as a necessary condition for one of the most important changes: a switch from the strategy of import substitution to outward-looking development.

BOD: I have already expounded my opinion on the 'shock therapy versus gradualism' debate on several occasions.[2] My belief that a once-and-for-all 'purgatory' is not a suitable method for the erection of the new system already became firmly established at the time I was working in the original MDF programme. My views were influenced by experience gained in the twenty countries I had by then visited, which suggested the following: there are certain universal institutions necessary for a market economy, but these are still not developed in my country, and there are certain specific existing features (resource combinations, institutions, traditions, values) that could come in useful, and that it would be a shame to bulldoze away. No matter how they come into being, a minimum of market institutions (clear-cut property rights, a functioning system of financial mediation, adequate

2 See 'Gradual Reform Works, Says Hungarian Official', *IMF Survey*, February 1992; 'Transition to a Market Economy in Hungary: The Role of the Financial Institutions', *Aula* (Budapest), 1992, No. 1.

financial discipline) is the necessary precondition of successful stabilization. If these institutions cannot be 'imported' as
in East Germany, then stabilization can be implemented only
step-by-step, always bearing in mind the current state of
institutional development and the capabilities of the institutions.

One of the arguments of the advocates of 'shock therapy'
is worthy of consideration: there is a danger that the measures of 'reform by instalment' do not reach the critical mass
necessary for real change. This consideration was indeed the
case of the partial reforms during the reform communist era.
In 1990, however, the question of real change was decided:
there was to be a change of system.

Another argument has also been considered within the
Hungarian government, which goes more or less as follows:
we are now shaping the entire institutional system of the
economy, but not all the economic variables have reached
their optimal values. In these conditions the new institutions
will evolve under wrong economic signals (such as relative
prices) and therefore they will operate less than optimally
right from the beginning. The recommendation was therefore
to set the optimal values in one go (one-go macroeconomic
stabilization) and let the new institutions of a market
economy evolve afterwards.

In my view, it was not errors of economic policy but
institutional factors that caused the sub-optimal variable
values, leading to the recurrent need for macroeconomic
stabilization in a command economy. For instance, price
distortions were partly the result of efforts by the large state
enterprises to restrict competition, hence anything that will
strengthen competition will also imply the modification of
prices (and naturally also of resource allocation) in the
appropriate direction. In other words, institutional reform by
itself carries the potential for improving economic signals. In

Hungary, savers, employees, businessmen and consumers have essentially acquired the norms of a market economy within a very brief period. The economy oriented itself to the West European markets with a speed that seems astonishing in retrospect, and entrepreneurial activity also proved to be highly vigorous.

In the autumn of 1990, however, this perspective was not fully clear to the main decision makers, and the single, painful, surgical intervention in the economy also had its adherents. Since then, economic crisis has badly shaken all the countries of the region. Hungary suffered the least losses, and *not* because it had not yet taken the necessary steps: on the contrary, it is one of the first - if not actually the first - to implement the changes. I have no wish to decide the debate, but I am strongly convinced that the more gradual approach chosen was better for Hungary.

KLAUS: The 'shock therapy' versus 'gradualism' contro- versy was a wrong and false dilemma that to our great regret played an important role in determining our reform strategy. A gradualist approach to economic reform implied the pre- servation of old economic institutions, especially that of cen- tralized decision making about investments, imports and, of course, pricing. Advocates of a gradualist strategy promised that they would be able to 'steer' the economy towards a market system more slowly and without social costs and that they would be able to keep the whole reform process under control.

Our reform strategy, based on radical deregulation and rapid privatization, was misleadingly named 'shock therapy' by our opponents and by their foreign advisers. But in spite of warning against the supposed dangers and social costs of 'shock therapy', its results are much better than those of the gradualist reforms in some other former communist countries.

In the overall conception of the reforms, were you thinking, as a strategy, of the need for confrontation with the main forces in the system such as state enterprises, trade unions, bureaucrats, or were you planning a strategy of cooperation (even at the expense of efficiency) – trying, for example, to rely on managers, workers' councils and public servants to carry out the reforms?

BALCEROWICZ: In designing the reform I was following what I saw as economic logic which, I believed, had a deep social significance going beyond the interests of the respective pressure groups. So I was trying to avoid the compromises that would make the programme more acceptable to some of them but at the cost of impairing its economic rationale. I preferred the risk of rejection of economically sound policies to the risk of economic failure of policies which would be socially acceptable but would make less economic sense. My view was that, given the very difficult economic situation (characterized by hyperinflation and shortages) and the sense of newly gained political freedom, people might expect drastic actions. This was strengthened by the belief that the existing and not yet fragmented political parties were still ready to think and to act in the name of the common good. (As a matter of fact, the radical economic programme was accepted at the end of December 1989 by the overwhelming majority of deputies from all the parties.)

In designing the economic programme I assumed that it would appeal to those who could make use of new opportunities and who could meet new challenges (new private entrepreneurs, more energetic and competent managers of state enterprises, professionals), while providing protection for those negatively affected, via the newly built social safety net, but to the extent and in the forms that were compatible with the essence of the economic programme. But I had no illusion that protection could be sufficient to avoid dissatisfaction on the part of some groups – workers from large state enterprises facing bankruptcy, for example.

With respect to the unions, in Poland they have been much more powerful than in Hungary or Czechoslovakia. According to the law on the trade unions, the government had a legal duty to consult the trade unions about all legal acts that affected standards of living – most of the economic measures, in other words. This was done in late 1989 and subsequently in a basically non-confrontational manner, but without compromising their economic rationale.

I realized that the institutional structure of the inherited economic system was unbalanced, given the presence of the strong trade unions, and I took some measures to strengthen the consumer organizations. I was also very much interested in the development of the employers' associations. The key to changing thebalance between interest groups was, to my mind, privatization, which would change the institutional structure of the labour market.

BOD: The economic sections of the programmes contained no considerations that could be described as political tactics because the underlying social policy assumption was that the vast majority of Hungarian society deemed the existing system to have no prospects. It could also be assumed that the better-informed strata of society were familiar with the requirements of, and the phenomena accompanying, a market economy. In practice, we did not need to reckon with resistance in the form of sabotage, violence or the organiza- tion of large-scale strikes. There was no doubt that the managers of the large enterprises that were to be privatized, reorganized or closed down had little sympathy for the change in regime, and there were concerns about the resistance of the large-scale industry lobby. With the collapse of the establishment party, however, the influence of the managers of large-scale industry weakened. It was an irony of fate that those 'socialist' industries that were the worst hit by this change were based on Soviet inputs or Soviet markets (metallurgy, machine industry) while the firms orienting themselves towards the west at least had a chance of survival.

The majority of trade union leaders did not show much sympathy either, even though they did acknowledge the need for a change in the economic system. According to public opinion polls, the trade union as a social institution was the least appreciated and the least popular institution; moreover, their energies were, for a long time, tied up in disputes among the various trade union organizations. In Hungary, the leading position of the former 'state' trade unions was not shaken by workers' councils or by alternative trade unions. Thus, in contrast to Poland, there was no politically strong labour movement at the beginning of the transformation. This circumstance reduced the chances of political confrontation but increased the resistance to economic measures.

As far as the social structural aspects of the issue were concerned, the entire programme attempted to keep corporatist tendencies at a distance. The fundamental consideration was that, at a time of rapid restructuring, entrepreneurial boom and necessary bankruptcies, the state need not press for corporatist structures 'from above'. Recent developments indicate, however, that, as the managerial stratum is transformed and becomes stronger, as the cooperation between the various industrial chambers and government agencies and between these chambers and the political parties becomes stronger, and as trade unions become more active in response to rising unemployment, the scope for governing free of corporatist interests shrinks. With many interest-representing organizations competing against one another, interest reconciliation will gain in importance in government policies.

KLAUS: Our strategy was to get the necessary support of as many citizens and of as many interest groups as possible. We knew that social consent was absolutely unavoidable for such a complicated process to be carried out, especially if the transformation required considerable sacrifices: a fall in real incomes and consumption, structural changes in production, the appearance of unemployment, and so on. We succeeded in creating a basic consensus with trade unions and, I would say, general consensus with employees, and so we avoided debilitating strikes. At the same time we rejected the idea of workers' councils in the firms, the relics of previous attempts at *perestroika* reform. Of course, there were and are interest groups, such as management of the largest state companies in heavy industries, that have been showing no interest in supporting our reform strategy, which would deprive them of the privileges they had under the old system. We did not want to have their support at any price. The basic principles of the reform strategy were more important to us, and we did spend a lot of time defending and explaining the reform blueprint to the population of the country and used its support as a defence against opponents of the reform. But it is interesting to point out that most opponents came from intellectual, academic circles rather than from the old-style bureaucracy.

Were you mainly thinking in terms of 'very best' policies, or of a more pragmatic set of measures that, although improving the existing system, would not lead to the most efficient outcome? If the latter is the case, was that because of a sense of realism about implementation capabilities or rather because of concern about the social costs involved in some of the 'very best' policies?

BALCEROWICZ: In designing and implementing the economic programme, I was guided by a vision of a 'good economy', as described earlier: a dominant private sector, competition, a liberal foreign trade regime with an outward-looking orientation, stable money, market prices, a limited but efficient state, and so forth. This was my concept of the 'very best' and I tried rather hard not to compromise it by giving in to pressures – for example, pressures from the farmers' organizations to introduce agricultural policies of the EEC type or pressures from the workers' lobbies to introduce wide-ranging preferences for employees' ownership in the process of privatization. I was particularly against measures that could satisfy some interest groups but at the cost of introducing largely irreversible and bad mechanisms. Again, agricultural policy of the EEC type was an example here. I had also been very much aware that one of the greatest dangers could be to set in motion a negative demonstration effect: by giving some concessions to one enterprise or branch one could set in motion a wave of pressures. This is why one of my main goals was to keep the policies as uniform as possible. This was also the reason I was very much against the constant demands to introduce an 'industrial policy' or 'microeconomic intervention' – in other words, widespread and detailed interventions into the affairs of enterprises.

BOD: Realities, or social costs, need to be taken into account right from the very beginning, as a kind of a constraint, in which case there is no 'very best' or 'second best' solution. However, the existence of the political or social costs did not frighten the decision makers away from adopting unpleasant measures. The pragmatic approach had already been embodied in the selection of the objectives. Considerations of political acceptability have always played a part (and still do) in the *timing* of the measures: many necessary measures were introduced belatedly, or with partial compensation. A few steps are bound not to be taken at all. What is of real importance is that no *retreat* takes place as a consequence of political pressure that could undermine the credibility of the government.

KLAUS: I never thought in terms of 'very best' or 'second-best' policies. It is a theoretical, unrealistic construction. We knew that neither a perfect reform strategy nor an optimal set of policies can be invented in advance and then simply introduced. First of all, the process of transformation from a communist system to democracy and a market economy is unique and there is no experience from which we could learn. It is therefore impossible to think in terms of a 'very best' blueprint, but we were forced to learn by doing. Second, we were concerned about social consensus, and the creation of a suitable social safety-net was one of the preconditions we had in mind when we formulated our reform strategy. But I don't think it is possible to compare various reform strategies in terms of social costs, because you cannot measure them. The critics of 'shock therapy' showed much concern about its social costs, without considering the social costs of non-reforms, of continuous resource misallocation and bad investment, and of macroeconomic instability. These social costs would surely be much higher.

3. Expectations, Economic Results and the Importance of Political Support

This chapter continues the account from the time prior to the launching of the reforms through to the implementation process. The discussion revolves around two major themes: the ways in which results coincided with the expectations held prior to launching the reforms, and the evolution of support for and opposition to the reforms. Regarding the first theme, the reformers discuss their expectations of the effects of the reforms, particularly in the face of the possible risks. They relate these expectations and plans to the way in which they implemented those measures, describing what factors needed to be incorporated in the course of the implementation process. In terms of the second theme, the reformers elaborate on the changing role of political support for and opposition to the implementation process and also the changing constitution of political support and opposition over time.

The three reformers provide a range of responses in discussing their expectations before to the reform. Klaus of Czechoslovakia was the most optimistic of the three as they faced the reforms, basing his optimism on his 'strong conviction that creating conditions for the market to work and for private initiative to flourish can accomplish the economic and social configuration better than any imaginable masterminded plan'. While he recognized that there were enormous uncertainties, Klaus believed in the ability of the Czech people to adjust. Bod of Hungary, on the other hand, paints a

much grimmer picture of the 'lasting and unsolvable problems' that he found himself facing as Minister of Industry
and Trade in 1990; according to Bod, the problems required
making what he knew would be 'unpopular' decisions, such
as the previous government considered politically too difficult to implement. Bod did however attempt to remain optimistic, as he understood that the restructuring process occurring in Hungary was not altogether unique. His greatest
worry was the public perception of these measures and their
effects: 'The general public had a different experience of
this bitter transition. Those hit by the crisis – the employees
of the companies going bankrupt, the former beneficiaries of
the socialist welfare state – have not heard much about
comparative economic history.' Balcerowicz of Poland also
confronted a large number of objective uncertainties that
could make it difficult to sustain the chosen programme,
particularly given the unknown magnitude of effects that the
reform measures would cause. However, his worst fear was
'to preside over an economic programme which was politically acceptable but failed because of not being sufficiently
radical and consistent'. Balcerowicz argued that even though
there was great uncertainty concerning the success of the
reform programme, the most feasible strategy for restructuring the economic system in Poland was through the implementation of the radical measures that he outlined in the
previous section; less radical measures might not have very
destabilizing economic and social effects in the short run,
but might be detrimental in the long run. He viewed his task
as pushing through this radical strategy, which he considered
to be Poland's most feasible option.

One of the factors that affected the implementation of
reform was the balance of supporters and opponents of these
programmes. In this chapter reformers discuss the bases of
support and opposition and how they evolved, including as

well how they tried to inform and influence public opinion. Interesting distinctions emerge in their discussions of the issue of communication with the public. The fact that these reform measures would effect what Bod has described in the previous pages as 'unpopular' short-term outcomes rendered public communication a key issue in mustering continued public support for the reform programme. In all three countries, political and popular support was high at the moment of political transition and the launching of the reforms, the period that Balcerowicz has described as the time of 'extraordinary politics'. The three reformers relate how they 'marketed' their reform programme, and what bases of support they focused on. While all three of them affirm the necessity of keeping the public informed about the nature of the reform programme and the expected effects of its measures, varying circumstances affect their media relationship with different strata of the public.

The constituency of public support was defined in large part by the balance of political power that initially supported the implementation of economic reforms. In Czechoslovakia, for example, the new government that replaced the hard-line regime in December 1989 called for immediate parliamentary elections, which it won with strong majorities in both national councils and in the federal assembly. This base, along with the complete delegitimization of the communist party, provided very strong support for complete economic restructuring. In addition, Václav Klaus made it a priority to cultivate a grass-roots political party that would be an informed basis of support. He was thus able to have political and public support converge on his behalf, and this constituted the basis of the Civic Democratic Party that helped to elect him as prime minister in the June 1992 elections.

This was not the case in Poland, however. The negotiated transition of 1989 meant that the old communist regime still

had representation in parliament, which constituted a significant institutional opposition. Balcerowicz's reform programme initially enlisted enough support across parties to
pass the necessary economic legislation, but a special and
concerted effort was needed to preserve political and popular
support as the effects of 'shock therapy' reform made themselves felt. The stabilization and liberalization measures left
farmers and workers – who constituted the broad base of
support for the transition as part of the Solidarity trade union
movement – increasingly dissatisfied, having expected more
help from the government. Popular discontent with the consequences of shock therapy combined with growing legislative opposition to mount pressure for a reversal of policies.
While Balcerowicz tried to build up public support through
direct communication with the public through TV broad-
casts, six months after the launching of the stabilization
programme monetary and fiscal policies were temporarily
somewhat relaxed.

While, as in Poland, Hungary's case was also one of a
negotiated transition of power, the Hungarian situation was
quite different for a number of reasons. First, unlike in
Poland and Czechoslovakia, there was no package of shock
treatment measures implemented by the newly elected
government. However, there were harsh economic measures
– which Bod describes here as 'unpopular' – that had
needed to be implemented and that elicited strong public
opposition. Bod recounts the incident of the raising of fuel
prices by 65 per cent, which precipitated a massive strike of
taxi drivers, such that the government had to halve the price
increase. Secondly, the Hungarian government historically
had a difficult relationship with the media that made inform-
ing the public and gaining public trust an extremely difficult
task. The strength of popular discontent made the lack of
public support and misinformation a greater hindrance to

implementing reform than did organized political opposition. Political opposition, according to Bod, was in fact inconsequential, as the elections had fixed the political relationship between political parties in parliament for four years.

Could you please elaborate in some detail your expectations concerning the effects, consequences and results of the reforms at the time they were launched? Were you, in general, an optimist or a pessimist? Was your general attitude enthusiastic or subdued, in view of the great risks facing your programme?

BALCEROWICZ: I perceived some uncertainty about the possibility of implementing and sustaining the chosen strategy. But my task in accepting both the job of Deputy Prime Minister and that of Minister of Finance was to push through the radical strategy, as the positions did not in themselves hold much attraction for me. So my attitude was that if it turned out to be impossible I would resign, and I certainly would have done so. The worst possible scenario was for me to preside over an economic programme which was politically acceptable but failed because of not being sufficiently radical and consistent.

What I had in mind as a warning was the fate of Raul Alfonsin in Argentina who started a radical stabilization programme as a very popular politician and who lost both the popularity and the stabilization. This is why I tended to prefer those policy options which were associated with a higher risk of being rejected by society but which, if implemented, promised to bring better economic results than those that were socially less risky but economically also less promising.

There were some specific concerns about the working of the respective mechanisms. Perhaps the single most important source of perceived uncertainty was the convertibility of the Polish zloty, which we decided to introduce at a low level of foreign exchange reserves. This is why it was so important to obtain the one billion US dollars of the stabilization fund. It turned out that it was not necessary, but this we knew only after the fact. Much uncertainty was also associated with the development of the budgetary situation after launching the economic programme. We expected a deficit in the first half of 1990; instead we got a surplus.

Practically all the important economic variables were subject to great uncertainty. For example, there were conflicting hypotheses about how fast the initial large price increases would spread across the economy; in other words what the inflation path would look like. I did not know how long we should be able to keep the stable exchange rate at its initial level. We were uncertain when and on what scale the bankruptcies of enterprises would occur. They started later and on a smaller scale than we had expected. We forecast a moderate growth of exports in 1990. In fact they exploded, growing by 43 per cent.

On the other hand I was reasonably certain about the general directions of change, that is, the general relationships between the policy measures and the changes in the economic variables, the time lags between the two and the magnitude of the reaction. Therefore I was sure that the stabilization and liberalization package, if maintained, would stop hyperinflation and eliminate shortages. I was also sure that sooner or later privatization of the economy, competition and export-oriented growth would bring about greatly enhanced efficiency; in other words, it would solve the perennial problem that plagued the former socialist economy.

BOD: Before elaborating on my expectations, I will provide some background information on the situation in my country at the time I took office. By 1988–89, it became evident to the politically aware public that state socialism was incapable of development and would, sooner or later, collapse. The only question that remained was the nature of the transition: would it be prolonged and full of bad compromises, or violent, or based on consensus? In Hungary, the issue seemed to depend primarily on the behaviour of the Soviet Union and only secondly on the national *nomenklatura* officialdom. However, at the end of 1989 it became evident that the Soviet Union accepted the fact of free elections. The elections, as is well known, brought defeat to both successors of the communist establishment party. After the elections it became clear that a coalition government had to be formed. This state of affairs foreshadowed a good many difficulties among the ruling parties as well as between the ruling and the opposition parties, and, more broadly, between those who were willing to face the new challenges and that part of society which had become resigned and turned distrustful.

As I took office in the new government as Minister of Industry, I found that the ministry was facing lasting and, in the ordinary sense of the term, unsolvable problems. The scope of the ministry encompassed industry, energy, domestic trade, the construction industry and tourism. It was not as if the condition of industry or the doom awaiting the traditional sectors had been a novelty for me. But the state of the ministry was such that – in contrast to those responsible for infrastructure or for economic policy functions – even if we had attained effective control over the situation, for two or three years there was nothing to be expected but reduction, closing down, winding up. In the areas under the Ministry of Industry, years would be needed for a positive turn to be perceptible – and even then, what would be required is enhanced quality, not merely renewed growth. Nevertheless, in view of some of our comparative advantages - primarily those of the relatively high qualifications of the labour force, traditional Hungarian industriousness, together with relatively low wages and a functioning material, legal, financial and other human infrastructure that surpasses what is available to our eastern neighbours - there was hope for the medium term. As far as trade was concerned, problems on the scale of those of industry have not appeared.

In retrospect all of this seems to have been easier than during the launching of reforms, when minor and major crises took their turns. I had to adopt a whole series of unpopular measures: dismissing fifty or sixty managers at the 120 large enterprises under the supervision of the minister, winding up firms of long standing. (The Széchenyi plaque that I received from the engineers of the Óbuda Shiyard, founded over 150 years ago by Count István Széchenyi, is still on my desk - but I was not in a position to save the company.) The first months were a time of tremendous daily tensions.

Nevertheless, I managed to view the difficulties in a realistic, almost optimistic light; also I managed to avoid emotional involvement at the time of crisis. The reason for this may have been that, on the basis of my reading and limited personal experience of developments in industrialized and the newly emerging industrial countries, it was quite clear to me that the process taking place in Hungary was not extraordinary in all respects. The painful restructuring, the decay of traditional industry, the market reorientation, the opening-up and outward-looking economic policies following autarkic periods - these were all concepts that could be amply studied in the economic histories of other countries. My professional background was of great help to me here. The general public, of course, had a different experience of this bitter transition. Those hit by the crisis - the employees of the companies going bankrupt, the former beneficiaries of the 'socialist welfare state' – have not heard much about comparative economic history. And even if they had heard of foreign examples, it would still not have soothed their disappointment.

KLAUS: My optimistic expectations about the reform were based on my strong conviction that creating conditions for the market to work and for private initiative to flourish can accomplish the economic and social transformation better than any imaginable master-minded plan. My optimism resulted from my belief in the ability of our people to learn, to change their patterns of behaviour and to adjust their activities rationally and voluntarily if the market provides the right incentives. However, the uncertainties were enormous. Despite forty years of distorted and rigid price structures, my optimistic expectations regarding price liberalization were based on the deeply rooted financial conservatism in our society at the level of the government as well as of the household. The actual results in this area were not very much different from my expectations. After liberalizing some 85 per cent of prices at the beginning of 1991, the initial price jump was about 50 per cent during the first quarter, but then the monthly inflation rate fell rapidly to almost zero in the middle of the year, and since then has been exhibiting very comfortable levels of approximately 1 per cent monthly.

The introduction of internal convertibility created fears about the appropriate exchange rate arrangements as well as about the exchange rate level. Our international reserves were minimal at that time and there were strong expectations of a devaluation, and speculation on that score among the business sector and the general population. We urgently needed to have a sustainable exchange rate level to anchor prices that were liberalized at that time. But since radical devaluations tend to fuel inflationary developments, there was a danger of a vicious circle of successive devaluations. But we took the risky step, devaluated the currency and pegged the rate to a basket of the five convertible currencies of our main trading partners. This measure proved to be absolutely right and since then the exchange rate has not been under any pressure despite some domestic inflation. Our international reserves are now at the highest level in our postwar history and cover comfortably six months' imports.

What exceeded even my optimistic expectations was the development of the private sector and the enthusiasm of the people to participate actively in privatization and to engage in business activities. The trade sector is now almost fully in private hands and three-quarters of the adult population are participating in the voucher privatization, investing either directly or through spontaneously established private invest-ment funds. Voucher privatization, despite scepticism abroad, proved to be both technically and politically feasible as well as highly successful compared to traditional, less controversial methods of privatization. Another method, the restitution of property to previous owners expropriated by the communists, proved to be unexpectedly productive. It accelerated the process of privatization and because of the relatively limited volume of property involved did not signi-ficantly complicate the whole process. These developments have produced major qualitative results, perceived by the population as a substantial improvement of their quality of life, and hence they increase public support for the reform.

What was your overall approach in communicating about the reforms? Did you try to encourage the public by express-ing high confidence in the success of the effort or did you try instead to deflate expectations by presenting a sombre scenario? Did you make optimistic or pessimistic press statements at the time? In general terms, should one be realistic even if this means giving a grim picture and creating anxieties, or should one induce positive expectations even if they are bound to be disappointed? What sort of message should the government try to present?

BALCEROWICZ: In my public pronouncements I rather tried to avoid unconditional forecasts, preferring statements along the lines, 'if ... the programmes hold, then ...'. Within this conditionality, I tried to give a realistic and rather general assessment of the prospects for a resumption of economic growth. (It turned out that I erred on the side of unintended optimism with respect to 1991.) I think, partly with the benefit of hindsight, that in this respect it is better to err on the side of pessimism with respect to economic growth. Otherwise the political opponents of the reform would use the negative discrepancy between the forecast and the reality as a proof that the whole programme was basically flawed. This is more dangerous than to have a political dispute about the programme based on a pessimistic forecast with respect to output.

But as far as statements, direct or indirect, about future inflation are concerned, my view has been to avoid very precise forecasts; but if one is to err at all, then one should err on the side of optimism. For I consider that the loss of credibility if the forecasts were to prove too optimistic is less harmful than fuelling inflation by making pessimistic forecasts. This was one of my major points of contention with one of the ministers who made what I regarded as some very unwise statements with respect to future inflation, probably in the belief that it was better for the sake of his reputation as a former academic economist to turn out to have been too pessimistic rather than too optimistic.

The marketing of the reform package is very important, but it should take the form of a serious discussion with the public rather than crude and simple 'salesmanship'. However, such a discussion is rather difficult, given the time limitations of the policy makers, and its effects are bound to be reduced if, as in Poland, there are powerful opposing communication campaigns linked to elections in the early phases of the economic programme. In any case there is a serious need for public education via the mass media, especially television.

BOD: What I regard as the most important in terms of the social preparation for economic change is that the 'marketing' of government measures should press two strong ideas on the public. First, that the transition is not unprecedented internationally, so we know the effects and mechanisms of most of the tasks; certain nations have faced these challenges successfully, others less so. We have a good chance of success. The second point deals with the familiarity of individuals, families, the professions, and small communities with the institutions, ethics and techniques of a market economy; the new legal concepts; the individual development mechanisms; and especially the successful examples and the reasons for cases of failure. This media work is naturally in the interests of the government – but also of the opposition, which hopes to win executive power at the next elections and would be in a better position if faced with an informed and motivated society. And it is in the interest of all those, irrespective of their political commitment, who wish to live in a more modern and more harmonious country. These tasks were not easy in the case of Hungary.

Following the general elections there was a view, that was vigorously expressed in the press, according to which the new government did not sincerely disclose the state of the nation in all its gravity to the country; furthermore, that the government was unable to keep its election promises.

To understand the circulation of this view, a few words should be said about the Hungarian press and mass media. In the last days of the reform communist regime, there was one sector in which privatization was accomplished: this was the printed media. The political dailies with the widest circulation were quickly transferred from state ownership, generally with the participation of foreign partners. The daily with the largest circulation, *Népszabadság*, formerly the 'central organ' of the establishment party, remained a 'socialist daily'; the daily of the trade unions, *Népszava*, has also shown little sympathy for the government; the semi-official paper of the previous government, *Magyar Hírlap*, also stands doubtless closer to the previous government than to the former Antall government. In addition, radio and television – which had been subjected to strict control by the establishment party until the eve of the collapse of the communist system – immediately perfected its independence *vis-à-vis* the government (that is, *vis-à-vis* the new government).

This background should be taken into account when analysing the public reception of the difficulties that accompanied the democratic changes. The problem is not that the government coexists with a highly critical press that in the main professes to ideologies and values different from its own. What is particularly strange is that, according to recent surveys, 90 per cent of the journalists have admitted to having party sympathies. Under the conditions of such a high degree of politicization, sufficient objectivity can be hoped for only if vigorous professional ethics, self-control or some other guarantee enforces it. That is not yet the case in Hungary. From the perspective of our subject, what is to be noted is not that the majority of the opinion-shaping media addresses the issue of the operation of the government with

a critical tone: what does cause a problem is that the government programmes do not easily get through to the citizens,
and, if they do, this is largely in a critical context. For this
reason, citizens know less than is necessary about the concepts of a market economy and about the measures taken by
the government.

As a result of the political press, at the time of preparing
this analysis (early 1993), the 'average Hungarian citizen',
according to public opinion polls, is highly critical of the
operation of virtually every institution, and assesses his own
as well as the country's position in the most pessimistic
terms.

KLAUS: It is absolutely necessary for the reformers to be
confident in the success of the reform, to inspire all supporters and to create broad pro-reform coalitions. The reform is
not an academic problem, it is a political issue and it is
vitally important to win political support for the reform programme. I realized from the very beginning that building a
political base for the implementation of our radical reform
was an indispensable component of all my activities. We
succeeded in creating the only conservative party in former
communist countries which is able to address the people
nationwide and that has national grass-roots political support. It required enormous political activity and hundreds of
political rallies in the country, meeting thousands of people,
speaking in hundreds of local meetings. Professional political campaigning, a specific public relations policy and deliberate image-building are an integral part of such activity.
What is essential for winning long-term popular support for
the reform is to have a credible programme. I would like to
stress here the necessity of avoiding any form of populism,
of giving any false promises of an easy way of reform. I
repeatedly argued that the devastation of our country was so

great that no one could expect rapid improvements, that reform has its inevitable pains and requires quite large sacrifices from the people. Telling the truth was a major asset which helped us to win the elections. It is important to promote self-confidence and a sense of responsibility for themselves among citizens accustomed to pervasive state paternalism. Our optimism, based on self-confidence and individual responsibility for the future, was the main argument which addressed the people and it helps us to proceed.

In your view, what were the major results *and the main* achievements *of the reforms? Please list only the two or three most important accomplishments and explain why you considered them crucial and central.*

BALCEROWICZ: In September 1989 Poland was struck by a number of serious economic 'diseases': extreme macro-economic instability (hyperinflation), massive shortages, low and falling efficiency, which was responsible for a declining standard of living. This was mainly due to the bad economic system.

There are, in my view, correspondingly major achievements of the Polish economic reform. Hyperinflation was halted, shortages are gone, and the quality and variety of goods on the market have radically improved. At the same time the economic system has been substantially trans-formed, and is now much more conducive to higher efficiency and economic development, which is more closely geared to economic welfare: that is not so wasteful as before. This has been achieved thanks to private property rights and the highest share of the private sector among the post-socialist countries (60 per cent of employment), the liberal foreign trade regime, free prices, convertible currency, a streamlined tax system, and so forth.

BOD: If, at the beginning of 1993, one looks back at the course of changing the social and economic regime, the historical perspective is still missing. What we today regard as successful may be shaken by tomorrow; what we today perceive as failure or an unsolvable problem may yet be settled. Matters of success and failure will be judged by a grateful or ungrateful posterity.

I regard the non-violent nature of the process as the most positive aspect of the change in systems, not only economically but in the widest possible sense; this has been a success for us all. If statistics can be believed, Hungary suffered a decline in output in the last three years comparable to that of the Great Depression of the 1929-33 crisis. Even if the decline was only half of that measured, the fact that social tensions have remained under control is remarkable.

Second, I would mention the successful and rapid change in economic roles: for example, the behaviour of households willing to make savings and to alter the structure of their consumption; or the manifestation of entrepreneurial skills. In one of the first interviews after the elections, I said that within two years we should have half a million entrepreneurs in Hungary: life fulfilled my forecast. The increase in the savings propensity of households, however, surpassed even the most optimistic forecasts; this was an important factor in curbing inflation and in effecting the general internal financial stabilization of the country.

Third, I regard the slow-down in the accumulation of external debt as of outstanding importance. It would have been very detrimental to the relaunching of the market economy in Hungary if it had begun with the cancellation of international financial agreements, or their renegotiation, and running after grants and forgiveness. In view of increasing exports and a GDP expected to grow again after 1993, the interest payment obligation, which is the real burden on the national economy, is relatively less and less of burden: we are slowly 'growing out of' the debt.

These achievements are a result of the implementation of a policy that enforced a strong microstructural transformation. The Law on Bankruptcy operating at full force; the policy of appreciating the exchange rate or at most remaining neutral towards it; the enterprise-by-enterprise privatization; the exposure of all sectors of the economy to import competition; the reduction of state subsidies and the elimination of cross-subsidization: all these factors have created pressure to adapt which does not seem to have been experienced in the other countries of the region.

While many outside observers have critically referred to this economic policy as Hungarian 'gradualism', these results show the marks of a consistent and tough policy, proving that the structure of the Hungarian economy has been irrevocably changed.

KLAUS: One of the most important results of our reform strategy is that we succeeded in maintaining a stable currency while deregulating most of the prices. After the jump in prices in the first quarter of 1991, the rate of inflation stabilized at a single digit level. Thus, we succeeded in creating a favourable market environment for rational behaviour on the part of all economic agents and for private enterprise as such. This is related to overall macroeconomic stability, particularly our ability to avoid deficit financing of the state budget. The second major result is that we completed the first wave of privatization through which we transferred most of our state-owned firms into the hands of private owners – individuals and private mutual funds. The transfer of control over firms was and is the main objective of our economic reform.

How much did the implementation *differ from the* original reform plan? *In other words, were policies changed in many substantial ways during the process of implementation? If so, was that due to (a) political pressures (even if you believed that economically the policies should not have been changed), or (b) the perception that there were indeed mistakes in the design that should be corrected as experience started to accumulate, or (c) changes in the external circumstances faced by your country?*

BALCEROWICZ: There were some important changes in the implementation compared to the original plan. But these changes were never intended to alter the general directions laid down in the plan. Rather they were responses to the divergences between the actual and expected results or circumstances, undertaken in order to maintain the general direction. Political pressures were never a decisive factor in making the adaptations; they played in some few cases a contributing role by signalling problems. The largest area of adaptive change was that of budgetary policy. In the middle of 1990, in view of the better than expected situation as regards the budget, the decision was taken to increase some expenditures, on housing and on the restructuring of dairies, among other things. In the latter case, the protests of the milk producers, performing a signalling function, played some role. But without the expected overall budgetary situation, these adaptations would not have been made, or quite certainly would have been much smaller.

In 1991 the situation in the budget turned out much worse than planned, mostly because of the much larger than expected decline of trade with Comecon and the related shock concerning the terms of trade. The action this time was taken mainly in order to reduce expenditures drastically; 80 per cent of the nominal revenue shortfall was thus absorbed.

In the middle of 1990 the central bank relaxed the monetary policy – excessively, as it turned out. The motivation for this was mostly economic: an assumed increase in the demand for money. But the previous decline in output may have played some role too, generating a desire to reverse this tendency. However, after it turned out that inflation rose again, monetary policy was quickly tightened despite the approaching presidential election.

BOD: In comparison to the 1989–90 programmes, certain processes have speeded up, bearing within them the marks of an unwanted shock solution. To begin with the external environment: the disintegration of the Soviet Union and its drastic weakening as a trading partner meant the loss of a natural market for many enterprises. I do not regret the disruption of relations that evolved under artificially distorted conditions, although the question of timing cannot be neglected even in the case of terminating a cooperation that is unsustainable in the long run. The rapid contraction of the enterprises of the former GDR is another example of drastically accelerated development. The Persian Gulf crisis (of 1990–91) caused oil prices to soar and our trading positions in the Near East to deteriorate at the most sensitive point in time from the point of view of the transition.

Internal factors had their part to play: the establishment and modernization of a number of institutions proved to be slower than estimated in the programme (examples are the new forms of state ownership, company improvement and venture capital investment activities, commercial banking services, the guarantee institutions for small business, and a number of institutional and legal aspects of land ownership). It is particularly unfortunate that a solution still cannot be found in some areas, as in the case of the construction and financing of housing.

The original programme proved to be too optimistic also with respect to the role of the local governments in organizing economic activity. I also believed that, with the abolition of the socialist 'council system', the new, autonomous local governments would release fresh energies through an active local tax policy and the rational utilization of their inherited assets (frequently quite substantial) through the mobilization of local resources. Some improvement has been achieved, especially in smaller villages, but mainly financed out of the central budget.

KLAUS: Our reform strategy was not a blueprint, dictating details and checking their fulfilment or perhaps failure. In these terms, there is no difference between the reform and its implementation. One of the main goals of our economic reform was to change the behaviour of our firms, to make them behave like true market agents. We knew that basically this is possible only through their privatization, but the privatization process takes some time. However, we needed to place the firms under a hard budget constraint so as to make them use material and human resources more rationally, and we did this by cutting subsidies and slowing down the growth of the money supply.

Unfortunately, external circumstances were not favourable for us: our firms were losing eastern markets and our exports were decreasing, which added greatly to the decline in our production. At the same time our firms did not show much readiness to accept the market rules of the game: customers with liquidity problems did not pay for deliveries and their suppliers went on delivering despite not receiving payments, which spread inter-enterprise indebtedness and insolvency throughout the economy.

As you have all pointed out, output declined markedly after the inception of the reforms. Can you give us your view of the main reasons for the decline in output? Were you worried by the rapid decline in production or were you aware that this was largely to be expected?

BALCEROWICZ: I approached the problem of the output decline in three stages. First, I realized that the official figures overstated the actual decline. The main reason for that was the inability to register the growth of the fastest-growing sector, that of small private enterprises. There were also problems with the estimation of inventories, and of changes in the range and quality of goods. The newest estimates done in the research institute of the Main Statistical Office confirm that the decline in output was grossly overstated; the new figure for the drop in GDP in 1990–91 is 5–10 per cent instead of the previous 18 per cent.

Secondly, I was aware that even the corrected figures for the reduction in GDP should be interpreted with caution, since part of the decline in output did not lead to a decline in general welfare. For example, sales of some basic foodstuffs in 1990 dropped by some 20 per cent while their consumption remained constant or even increased. The main reason for this discrepancy was a reduction in the waste of foodstuffs due to sharply increased prices and the elimination of shortages (the end of shortage buying, in other words). Another example of the reduction in the registered output, at least partly related to the reduction in waste, was the sharp drop in railway transportation services: the hardening of enterprises' budget constraint had led them to rationalize their transportation costs. Generally speaking, a portion of output in each socialist economy was 'pure socialist output': by definition this was an output that could have existed only in a socialist economy characterized by shortages, no competition, soft budget constraints of enterprises, and so forth. 'Pure socialist output' includes a certain level and type of production which is a counterpart of low efficiency. Moving away from socialism involves a decline in that output; conversely if there is no drop in 'pure socialist output' the economy is not moving towards the market system.

Third, with respect to the reasons for the decline in output besides the reduction of waste, there were, in my view, the following main determinants. The radical change in the systemic and macroeconomic environment of enterprises involved some adjustment costs. Some enterprises used their newly gained freedom in order to set prices at an excessively high level and then – given the tough macroeconomic environment – they reduced output. This strategy was helped by the fact that the financial reserves of many firms turned out to be higher than expected. The two election campaigns in 1990 and in 1991, with their sharp criticism of the economic programme, led to expectations that there might be a reversal in economic policies and thus contributed both to the delay in adjustment by enterprises and to wage pressure. Finally the collapse of trade with Comecon and the related terms of trade shocks were the most important reasons for the decline in output in 1991, but they had already started to operate in 1990.

I was worried above all about the political implications of the official (uncorrected) figures for output decline, for they were used by the political opponents of the programme to demand its radical revision, by way of a decisive relaxation of monetary policies, widespread state intervention ('industrial policy') and protectionism. In this they were supported by the majority of Polish economists and by some foreign ones. These demands had to be rejected.

BOD: If we examine the past three years from a statistical point of view, of the four possible evils (inflation, current account deficit, economic decline and unemployment), the decline of production and employment posed the gravest problems. I had not expected such a decline. As far as the growth of unemployment is concerned, I would emphasize two unexpected factors. One we should in fact rejoice in: the flow of foreign capital to the productive sector and the rapid modernization of the structure of production to a greater extent than expected. Joint ventures and companies held by foreigners quickly absorbed the labour force made redundant by modern technology, organization and incentives. In addition, they quickly drove state enterprises of similar production profiles from the market-place. These state enterprises used to be the largest employers. The other unexpected factor was the legislative spirit in relation to unemployment. I was surprised at how strong the support was, within all the parliamentary parties, for an undifferentiated – and hence costly – system of unemployment benefits. It is true, of course, that at first the difficult budget position was also not evident, so the burden of these benefits did not seem so large.

Today, I am less worried by the statistics showing the fall in production. On the one hand, there are increasing signs indicating that output is greater than what is registered in the new business sector because its activities are hard to capture by statistical monitoring (and by the tax authorities). It seems quite certain that the actual fall in GDP has been less than what has been measured: the data on electricity consumption, *inter alia*, indicate this.

Also, the higher than expected inflow of capital and new enterprises will increase production and export capacities at a fast pace in the near future. The restructuring and re-orientation towards the market, implemented more radically and faster than originally envisaged, caused at first a greater decline; but they also created sooner than they would have done the structure in which growth will be of a new type. What may be true of output and exports will not, however, apply to employment: the foreign companies will not employ hundreds of thousands, not even when working at full capacity; and domestic private businesses also operate under hard budget constraints.

KLAUS: The causes of the decline in production were both internal and external. External causes were largely expected. The collapse of eastern markets, especially those in the former USSR, brought about systemic shocks in our economy, because our exporters were far from able to find quickly in other countries new customers for their (mostly low quality) goods. The decline in their production was sharp and unavoidable, in spite of considerable devaluation of our currency. It was rather disappointing for us that West European countries responded to our troubles by offering only financial assistance (loans), instead of offering us the real assistance that we needed and still need: wider opening of their markets for our goods.

But, of course, there were internal causes of our production decline, too. Most important was the uncertainty of our firms and of their management about their future owners and future prospects, which discouraged them from investments and caused them to delay. Also, there was too great a squeeze on credit and I must admit that I am not fully content with the behaviour of our big banks and with the process of restructuring our banking industry. However, I must say that the decline in output was largely expected and that this is unavoidable in every economy undergoing transformation.

From which sources did the support for the reforms come and from where did the main opposition arise? What was the balance between support and opposition at the beginning, and how did it evolve?

BALCEROWICZ: The balance of support for and opposition to reforms was changing over time. The first phase was the phase of 'extraordinary politics': given the newly gained freedom and the dramatic economic situation, most of the people were ready to accept some drastic measures. The existing political parties were more inclined than normally to think and act in terms of the common good. It was in this atmosphere that a radical economic programme was discussed and adopted by all political parties in just ten days in late December 1989. As time went by and the programme started to bite, the opposition to it also grew. The most vocal protest came from the farmers' organizations, both from those linked to the former communist party and from those related to the former opposition. These protests can be partly explained by the fact that in 1989 the farmers achieved some windfall gains: the terms of trade improved sharply in their favour as prices of foodstuffs were liberalized, while the prices of inputs into agriculture were still controlled and heavily subsidized, and taxes were wiped out by hyperinflation. These extra gains were taken back in 1990 within the framework of the radical stabilization and liberalization programme. With the passage of time, the trade unions also became more aggressive, especially with respect to the wage controls. Therefore, more and more time had to be spent on negotiating with them and on defending the tough macroeconomic policies. By the time of the election campaigns in 1990 and 1991, most of the parties were trying to gain popularity on a populist platform.

On the other hand the radical economic reform had strong

support among the people with higher education, strongly represented in the pro-reform parties. Also, the entrepreneurs, whose number had been growing rapidly, were on the whole in favour of the market economy. People employed in the private sector, too, were on average more supportive than those in the state sector. Therefore, the rapidly growing share of the private economy outside agriculture has some positive political implications for the market-oriented reform.

BOD: When analysing the social support for the change of system, a sharp distinction must be made between the political institutions (government, parliament, political parties) and the principles that governed making the change. The popularity of the institutions sank rapidly and has remained low. In my view, this is related to the still widespread belief that it is first and foremost the minister, the party politician, the mayor – in general, the person representing public office – that is responsible for the state of the nation (in our case, for the state of the economy). According to public opinion polls, Hungarian citizens tend to view the state of the economy critically, and this leads to the general lack of popularity of politicians and, unfortunately, also of political institutions.

The principles themselves however, have not been seriously eroded. Surely, there are more opponents of privatization today than at the time when the process had not yet been launched and its side-effects could not yet be seen. But there is no sign of any strong feelings against, for example, the economic role of foreigners. Today, political parties tend to speak more about unemployment, poverty, the need for stimulating the economy than two years or even one year ago. Nevertheless, no considerable social force has formulated an alternative to the principles of a market economy. If, however, the advantages of the new structure do not soon become perceptible, the proportion of opponents to the changes would grow and the consensus built up around the market economy would weaken. It must not be forgotten that the decrease in wealth and incomes concomitant with such a substantial transformation makes every reform measure exceedingly difficult to implement. Transformation in itself is a shock to society, increasing its sense of insecurity. As the example of the modernization of Portugal or Greece shows, the building up of a modern competitive economy is a great trial even where there are satisfactory growth prospects. In our region, this transformation has been encumbered by the temporary contraction of the economy. It is therefore very important that this transition should be of short duration and that the public should also perceive it to be so.

KLAUS: Generally speaking, the opposition to our reforms came from the left wing of our political spectrum, not alone from our communist party, which is still the second strongest party in our parliament. Opposition to reforms came from the social democrats (and some other smaller left-wing parties) as well, because they are led by politicians of frustrated ambitions, who are disappointed that their concepts of reform have not been accepted. However, the majority supported our reform process from its very beginning. Of course, some people are dissatisfied with the decline in their living standard, but at the same time most of them understand that this is an unpleasant, but temporary, troubled period which is unavoidable for future prosperity. The result of our general election in 1992 confirmed that people in the Czech republic think, feel and believe in the beneficial results of our reforms in the future.

Can you tell us how you dealt with the opposition to reforms? What did you do to rally support? Is it important, in your view, to form a constituency that would actively support change? Did you make the formation of such a constituency a key goal of your policies? How much can or should be changed from the original plans in order to obtain political support at each point in time?

BALCEROWICZ: I tried to gain the political support for radical economic reform from all the political parties represented in parliament. This attempt was successful: the economic programme was discussed and adopted in December 1989 by a large majority representing all the political parties. Also, the trade unions, which had the legal right to be consulted about legislative proposals affecting living standards, did not put forward any major critical objections.

With the passage of time, criticism of the economic programme increased. Also, the split in the 'Solidarity' movement in 1990 and the related antagonism had made the general political atmosphere worse. But it was still possible, thanks to political consultations across party lines, to gain acceptance from parliament of all the major economic legislation proposed by the government, and to block any legislative proposals that would deviate from the government's economic programme. And this was done by a parliament where neither the Mazowiecki nor Bielecki government had the majority. This situation ended just before the parliamentary elections in October 1991, when an atmosphere of struggle dominated the political scene.

The formation of a constituency that would support economic change is obviously important. In Poland this constituency was largely represented by two main pro-reform parties: the Democratic Union of Tadeusz Mazowiecki and the Liberal Democratic Congress of Jan Krzysztof Bielecki.

There was obviously no need to organize another political party. With the help of my closest associate, Jerzy Kozminski, I created a non-party structure for the support of the economic reform, which was called 'Spring'. It was helpful in generating the political support for economic reform in parliament, as it grouped deputies from various political parties.

Generally speaking, if the original economic plan is correct, then the most one can do on political grounds is to delay certain measures, but only if this does not diminish their chances of adoption. In practice, however, the delay is likely to reduce the probability of the adoption of the necessary harsh measures, since the first period of 'extraordinary politics' is when the people are more likely to accept such measures. Consequently one should use such a period of 'extraordinary politics' to try to take as many difficult steps as possible.

BOD: Every programme has its beneficiaries and its losers, its supporters and its opponents – even a technocrat blind to politics is aware of this truism. He may not know, however, that one should never equate the beneficiaries of a programme with its supporters, nor its losers with its opponents. The transformation of Central and Eastern Europe demonstrates this. The new opportunities offered by a market economy benefited first and foremost the former ruling strata, owing to their advantageous initial position. It does not follow from this, however, that the former party secretary who is now a major merchant would support the new government. In addition, those who stand to lose by it, whether relatively or absolutely, could hardly be won over as supporters.

If all this is taken into account, we would be led to a somewhat pessimistic conclusion: namely, that if the change disadvantageously affects even a smaller but significant part of society, no lasting support can be won for major economic reforms, and particularly for a radical turnabout. Indeed, the experiences of the past two or three years in the region seem to support the following conclusion: the governments that have initiated radical change have either failed quickly or postponed the really unpopular measures for the sake of staying in office.

Even if our observations are pessimistic with respect to the survival of governments, the matter is not so hopeless as regards the direction of economic transformation. A government that is attempting to change the economic regime may fail; but, until now, forces that could have stopped or significantly reversed the process of transition to a market economy have not come to power anywhere in the region. For this process is driven by two major forces. One is the *pressure of the external world*, and the other is a negative force: there is *no convincing alternative programme*: a return to state socialism has not (yet) appeared even in the most desperate national communities. In any case, it is no accident that government changes have been so frequent in the region.

The Hungarian case differs from these tendencies on two major points. First, as a result of the hesitant *reform process* of the two decades preceding the change of system, the circle of individuals ready and willing to operate in accordance with the dictates of the market – and hence the range of potential beneficiaries – was wider than elsewhere. As discussed earlier, this does not guarantee greater support as well, but the process of establishing a market economy does take place in a more supportive environment if not simply the well-positioned have a real chance of acquiring property. The other specific feature is the *stable political system*, which, with a high degree of probability, guaranteed the exercise of executive powers for four years from 1990. Thus the system of parliamentary democracy has, in principle, already determined the changing power relations between supporters and opponents of the process for a term of four years.

As a result of this, Hungary has approached a state in which the question of supporting or opposing the change can be placed into the framework of the classical *political cycle*. What does distinguish the usual political processes from those of transitional economies, however, is the time taken for the implementation of the change and the social cost of that implementation. To put it simply: the transition to a market economy will, with absolute certainty, reduce the income-generating capabilities of the national economy and depreciate national wealth (or whatever had been considered national wealth) in the first phase; and the 'first phase' may extend beyond the term of office of a government. Thus the change in economic regimes shakes the absolute position of many, while its advantages become tangible later, and even then not for all.

At the time of expounding this analysis [early 1993], there is approximately one year left of the four-year government cycle. Hitherto, the decreasing support for economic measures seems not to have diverted the decision makers from their original course. There is no doubt, however, that the attention paid to political acceptability is reflected in their delaying a number of measures, including the reform of education and health care and, in general, the reform of public finances. Other examples are raising energy prices to the level of costs, which the government has been able to enforce in the case of large consumers but, when it came to households, welfare considerations proved to be stronger. Such political consideration is natural: similar phenomena can be observed in the case of the local governments, where unpopular measures are implemented only after lengthy deliberation, if at all.

KLAUS: As early as the first half of 1991 it was clear that there is no consensus in the Civic Forum, the major political movement that won the first elections after the revolution in the Czech republic, about our strategy for reform. The movement split into two parts: the right-wing Civic Democratic Party and the left-wing Civic Movement that would not compromise any longer over the reform strategy. This development was logical and unavoidable. I don't think it is necessary or possible to achieve a general consensus about the reforms and to maintain such a consensus at all costs and at all times. There always is, and always will be, left-wing opposition to market-oriented reforms and it will find its supporters among citizens who enjoy being taken care of by the state and who are afraid of a market environment. What is a key goal, and what, I believe, we have succeeded in achieving, is the formation of a political party that can devise a clear political and economic programme, that is able to address people and gain their support, without promising them what cannot be fulfilled.

How much were you trying to affect people's expectations after the reforms got under way? How did you communicate with the public regarding the results already obtained, future policies, and the costs and benefits ahead? In general, how important are both expectations and confidence in the outcomes of reform policies?

BALCEROWICZ: Before launching the radical stabilization and liberalization programme I concentrated on conditional forecasts: if the programme were accepted in practice, then inflation would be radically reduced and shortages would be eliminated. In my public statements, I continued to link the possible effects to our policy measures and to the changes in the economic system. Specifically, I tried to stress the link between the possibility of raising real wages and an increase in the general competitiveness of the economy, which is in turn a function of the privatization of the enterprises, an outward-looking orientation, competition, stable money, a limited but efficient state, and so on. I generally tried to avoid giving the exact timing as I knew that there was quite a lot of uncertainty and that time lags between the adoption of respective measures and their effects could not be foretold precisely. But there was constant pressure to commit 'the fallacy of misplaced concreteness', by saying exactly when the situation would improve and when the general standard of living would rise. I generally resisted these pressures in the interest of future credibility.

But the budget had to be based, according to the Polish law, on rather comprehensive and detailed economic forecasts with respect to output, profitability, inflation, balance of payments, wages, and so forth. Some of these forecasts unavoidably turned out to be wrong, and this was used by some opponents of the programme to claim that the whole scheme was basically flawed.

I communicated with society via the regular debates on the economy in the Parliament which were shown on TV. I also appeared on some TV programmes on certain special occasions, notably the launching of the radical stabilization and liberalization package in late 1989, or achieving the debt reduction from the Paris Club in April 1991. In Polish conditions, the efficiency of communication about the economic reform was reduced by the countervailing pre-election publicity campaigns of 1990 and 1991, during which Polish society was bombarded with strongly populist and demagogic messages. This dynamic of political events was a spontaneous process beyond the control of any single political actor. It was certainly not very fortunate from the point of view of communicating to the public the sense of a radical and comprehensive economic reform.

BOD: As far as people's expectations and the possibility of *influencing* these expectations are concerned, the basic formula of parliamentary democracies already holds for Hungary: it is not the executive power that determines public opinion, but vice versa. In this sense, the implementation of the system-changing programme by the government is taking place within the framework of political institutions and relations with the mass media. Naturally, political forces may produce illusions: they attempt effectively to manipulate expectations and opinions. The Hungary of transition – and this is certainly characteristic of the entire region – inherited not only underdeveloped market institutions, but also *underdeveloped political institutions*. Thus the political parties cannot rely on the historically conditioned support of their members. Hence, the lack of communication and the consequent apathy, lack of information, disinformation or misinformation constitute the greater problem, not political opposition. Open and dynamic communication could do a great deal for the acceleration of the learning process; I believe, however, that, because of the rapid change in the rules of the social and economic game, this process is going to be a long one.

The spreading of information and the creation of a business culture is a complicated process of *diffusion*. In the case of unskilled labour in traditional industrial districts, the process of understanding the logic of macroeconomic processes will be long and very difficult – especially as this group stands to lose by the process in several respects. By contrast, the entrepreneurial stratum quickly follows the changes and it demands continuous information. For this reason, the work of government agencies and that of the central bank and the other financial institutions should be strengthened: the provision of information and analyses can make the decisions of savers, investors, entrepreneurs, employees – in a word, all economic actors – easier.

KLAUS: Expectations are very important, as everybody who has studied economics knows, because they influence economic decision making and the behaviour of individuals and in this way they influence economic outcomes. Of course, we tried to influence people's expectations, and we did so by explaining to them what the goals of the specific reform steps were and what results could be expected from these steps. We expected a considerable jump in prices after the price deregulation, which would soon be followed by price stabilization. We devalued our currency considerably and promised future stability of the exchange rate. Our predictions came true. People did not stop believing in money and went on saving. Thus we did not allow high inflationary expectations to build up in our economy. The most important factor was that the government maintained its credibility and thus its ability to influence people's expectations of the future.

We always stressed the individual responsibility of every citizen for his future living standard, job opportunities and so forth, and we tried to promote entrepreneurial initiative and private business activity as the main source of future prosperity. We discouraged people, too, from relying on the government, from continuing with their passive habits of the past as well as their irresponsible attitudes towards their work and towards the community at large. We always try to tell the truth about the future: we try not to make false promises, promote false expectations and provoke false hopes about the government's ability to guarantee social welfare and future prosperity. I can say that up to now we have been quite successful in presenting the people with credible programmes and winning their support even though we have never made populist promises. We rely on the sound rational logic of the Czech people, traditionally sceptical about governments and their promises, on the deeply rooted individualism in our society, and on a long tradition of private enterprise.

The issue of people's expectations is closely connected with the ability of the reformers to communicate with society. We live in a democratic society with guaranteed freedoms and it also means that the anti-reform forces have great opportunities to influence public opinion and to promote anti-reform feelings and activities. The reformers must be more active than the anti-reformers in order to succeed. As I have said, economic reform is the hottest political issue and the reformers cannot sit in their offices and orchestrate the ideal sequence of reform measures. They must become politicians, create a powerful grass-roots political base for their policy, wage media campaigns defending the reforms and attacking their opponents. Only by doing this can the ordinary citizen be addressed. Such communication can be successful in the long run only if it is based on realism and truth. In that case there will be no discrepancy between statements and realities.

What were your major mistakes? Why were they made? Could they have been avoided or were they inevitable? (Alternatively you could answer this question by telling us if you could do it all over again, what are the main things that you would have done differently?)

BALCEROWICZ: I would not have changed anything essential in the economic strategy. This strategy has had many more chances for success and has displayed many fewer risks than alternative strategies that delay the stabilization and liberalization until deep institutional change has been advanced or those that propose gradual stabilization or liberalization (or both).

But there are a few things within the adopted radical strategy which with hindsight I would try to do differently. First, I would have tried to abolish sooner the inherited indexation of salaries in the budgetary sphere. The attempt to do it in 1991 met with political resistance in parliament and was only partially successful. Second, I would have tried to block the introduction in 1990 of the quarterly indexation of pensions. This later proved to be one of the sources of the problems in the budget and had to be reduced amidst political tensions. Third, the relaxation of monetary policies in the middle of 1990 turned out to be premature and excessive and had to be reversed.

BOD: The historical distance between this account and the events it is based on is not great enough to see clearly the mistakes made in the course of the drafting of the programme and its implementation. If possible mistakes are to be discussed, then we should consider first the assessment of the situation (the phase of the initial hypotheses), secondly the drafting of the programme (definition of objectives, allocation of economic instruments, the coherence of these instruments), and thirdly the analysis of the programme's impact and the implementation of corrections. This last phase could overlap with the phase of implementation and is the subject of eternal debates - particularly in the case of failure - over whether the original programme was mistaken or its implementation went wrong.

As a member of the new government, I took part in the

programme's implementation only for a year and a half, and as president of the central bank I am now responsible for a particular range of economic processes. If I were to ask what I would have done differently, I would hardly begin with the instruments or the goals; instead, I would start with a reassessment of the conditions.

Towards the end of 1989, and in early 1990, the authoritative economic and political opinions concerning the main components of the Hungarian economy's external environment were as follows:

1. Despite a rapid dissolution of the ties to the Soviet Union and Comecon, business relations of several decades' standing would enable a part – a fast decreasing part – of Hungarian products to find buyers in the eastern markets even under the new pricing conditions. (The typical example is the Hungarian IKARUS bus, of which some 70-80,000 units were used on the Russian roads – if the supply of spare parts alone is taken into account, this means a rationally irreplaceable link.) However, the economic disintegration and financial deterioration of the Soviet Union took place at such an unforeseen rate that the market loss of several years was condensed into a few short months.

2. We had no illusions about western aid, development assistance and market access, but the political gestures in 1989 did suggest more than what was actually realized in 1990-91. The negotiations with the European Community on an Association Agreement dragged on and western political intentions weakened in the meantime. This may have been motivated by the downward turn of the trade cycle in Western Europe and by the spreading of animosity towards foreigners (diminishing the chances of Hungarian workers taking up employment in Western Europe), and also by the fact that the process of democratization suddenly began to speed up also to the east of us, whereupon the number of countries to be supported increased.

3. Central European trade declined faster than expected, partly owing to the weakening of common interests and to the lack of elaborate mechanisms for a smoother transition, and partly owing to the unexpectedly brutal disintegration of other states (as in the case of Yugoslavia). External conditions evolved less favourably than expected. Thus an external shock much greater and much more intensive than was foreseen aggravated the difficulties inherent in a change of regimes.

With respect to internal factors, many of them turned out to be more favourable than originally assumed (for example, propensity to save, or willingness to take business risks). But institution development and economic legislation took longer than I expected. With the wisdom of hindsight, a number of issues should have been dealt with differently: in particular, more energy and attention should have been devoted to the erection of basic economic institutions (privatization, the financial system), even if this required setting up a separate government agency; and in terms of economic legislation, an accelerated procedure for the preparation and enactment of laws should have been fought for.

KLAUS: We have inevitably made hundreds of mistakes, but in my opinion none of them was of strategic importance. The biggest mistakes in my opinion were made in Czech–Slovak relations, where developments gradually resulted in the dissolution of Czechoslovakia. The mistakes that we made contributed, to a certain extent, to this process, but the Slovak desire to become a sovereign independent country was so strong and so deeply rooted that it could not be satisfied within the federation by any policy from Prague. These developments necessarily complicate our economic situation, but did not affect the reform itself. The actual results of the reform so far support our strategy and I would not make any substantial changes if I could do it again.

4. Prospects

In this final chapter Leszek Balcerowicz, Peter Bod and Václav Klaus discuss the state of affairs after the initial implementation of reforms and also the future economic prospects in their respective countries: what tasks lie ahead, what sorts of possible risks they envisage, and what sort of long-term development they chart for their respective countries compared with the standards of Western Europe. The chapter concludes with the advice that each of the three offers to colleagues in Russia and other former Soviet republics that are currently involved in drawing up and implementing similar economic reforms.

The three reformers each summarize the transition process so far as *successful*. They portray their respective countries as having weathered the political transformations as well as the initial effects of the macroeconomic stabilization process. However, they also agree that the fundamental structural reforms which are now under way need to continue, and that they imply far-reaching social, political and economic changes in the future.

Leszek Balcerowicz evaluates Poland's economic situation as fulfilling his vision of an efficient economic system, which as he mentions throughout these discussions is 'characterized by the dominance of various forms of private enterprise, an outward-looking orientation, competition, stable money and an efficient state which focuses on those functions it performs the best'. Of the three countries, Poland experienced the deepest economic crisis before it began implementing the reforms. Balcerowicz asserts, however, that Poland survived the shock of stabilization and liberalization. Certain tasks of stabilization still remain, as does the completion of numerous institutional reforms, including the privatization of large enterprises. The greatest risk that he foresees is the delay of these indispensable institutional reforms due to political or external pressure. This, in his view, explains the need for a strong democratic political system that can provide continuous support for institutional restructuring. The implementation of such restructuring is necessary for the country's continued economic growth, as is access to western markets.

Similarly, Peter Bod evaluates Hungary's state of affairs after what he terms the 'restructuring crisis of 1990–91'. He recounts that the economy began to stabilize in 1992, and he expects it to continue to do so; he does, however, identify the weakness of western economies and limited access to their markets as a negative influence. The greatest risks that Bod envisages for Hungary are the social tensions and political opposition that certain necessary structural reforms will elicit. While Bod does not foresee economic growth in Hungary reaching that of the 'small tigers' (the rapidly industrializing countries of Asia: Taiwan, Singapore, Malaysia, South Korea), he does forecast modest growth; the burden of restructuring the state apparatus will prolong the process of closing the gap with the west.

Václav Klaus sees the near future as bringing real economic adjustment at the level of firms, as the effects of the privatization process make themselves felt. The Czech Republic will also have to deal with the economic effects of the dissolution of the Czechoslovak Republic, as well as the disappearance of the former USSR as an economic power. Once the political situation is resolved and the framework for the operation of a market economy is in place, Klaus sees future projects focused on strengthening markets and increasing foreign investment. As long as there exists a strong and clear economic programme, Klaus asserts, the Czech Republic will continue its progress.

What, in your view, is the most serious risk facing the reforms? Is it populism, the return of communist influence, or a right-wing dictatorship?

BALCEROWICZ: Poland is well on the way towards a stable and competitive market economy. Prices are free, money is largely convertible, the private sector employs about 60 per cent of the total labour force, the switch is under way from import-substitution to outward-oriented growth and the role of foreign trade has radically increased. The supply of goods is now incomparably better than three or five years ago and the financial sector and local governments have learned a lot about how to operate in a market economy. But some important tasks remain. First, the inflation rate must be brought down to below 10 per cent annually. Second, the liberal nature of the present economic system should be maintained and defended against certain pressure groups. Third, some important institutional reforms have to be completed: these include the privatization of larger enterprises, the strengthening of the position of local governments, reform of the health services, and reform of the social security system. All these changes are needed in order to complete the construction of an efficient economic system in Poland, characterized by the dominance of various forms of private enterprise, an outward-looking orientation, competition, stable money and an efficient state which focuses on those functions that it can perform the best (such as providing a clear and efficient legal order, ensuring monetary stability, supplying public goods, and caring for education, health and the physical infrastructure). An efficient government should also refrain from engaging in activities in which it cannot be competent and which would induce massive rent-seeking (such as a wide-ranging industrial policy, manipulating the tax system and custom duties, heavy agricultural protectionism through the exclusion of agriculture from the operation of the market mechanism, and so forth).

To this vision of the efficient economy belongs also the strengthening of the democratic political system. This should include the implementation of a new electoral law, providing for more concentration in the party system, and a new constitution, which would set a clear and strict limit to irresponsible fiscal policies.

The most serious *risk* facing the reforms is the danger of slowing down some important measures, particularly the privatization of larger enterprises. There may also be attempts to return to selective protectionism and related rent-seeking.

BOD: At the present time we do not yet know the end of the story. I could summarize the facts about the transformation of my country in the following way.

The country has successfully performed the single, non-recurrent act of changing the political regime and of breaking away from the Soviet military, political and economic ties. The country meanwhile has remained operational. The grave external conditions and the unexpectedly dynamic internal processes, however, manifested themselves in a substantial economic decline and in the growth of unemployment. Even so, the decline has been relatively the smallest in the region. Still, the consequences of the decline were different from those envisaged in the original programme of the transformation of the economy, and this has had the effect of straining politics and the public mood, testing the ability of

Hungarian society to withstand social tensions. Towards the end of 1991 it became evident that the major price adjustment would not result in runaway inflation; in 1992, the stabilization of the economy began.

One of the determining elements of our prospects is the external environment. This gave us less than what we had hoped for. Owing to the weak upturn of the cycle in Western Europe and to the limited access to their markets, dynamic, export-driven growth is unlikely in the coming few years, although a positive growth rate was observed by the end of 1992. Internal processes are characterized by the modernization of the economy, but at rates different from region to region and from sector to sector. Because of these factors, there will be more to do than originally envisaged, in economic diplomacy as well as in the operation of internal equalizing mechanisms.

The major restructuring crisis of 1990–91 speeded up the growth of the tertiary sector: the shares of agriculture and industry have been declining fast, while that of services has been on the increase. The economy has taken on a markedly dual nature, with the appearance of large multinational companies (car manufacture, pharmaceuticals, the food industry) on the one hand, and the emergence of thousands and thousands of small businesses on the other. This structure is beginning to look like that of southern Germany and northern Italy. In terms of the budget, the problems include weaknesses in taxation and employment, the still socialistic nature of the welfare systems, and the lack of initiatives in levying taxes or in the privatization of municipal assets on the part of many local governments.

Regarding the sources of danger, I would like to say that, although the democratic institutions have lost popularity, they have remained strong. The widening of the income gap and political apathy may strengthen the anti-market, communistic forces that proved to be marginal in the 1990 elections: the political scene in Hungary's immediate neighbourhood clearly shows that these forces exist. However, I would not give much of a chance either to a return of the old *nomenklatura* or to anti-market demagogy. Following the critical shift in 1990–91, by 1994 about a half of the households should find their place within the framework of the new economic system. As for those who will not have been able to find their place within the market economy or to find a common ideology or positive programme, most of them do not take part in the political life of the country anyway. This is, of course, a dangerous social formula, which the government will have to address by way of a selective welfare and regional policy, retraining and education.

KLAUS: It is very difficult to provide prognostic scenarios for the long term. We are living on a day-to-day basis and a two-month period ahead seems to us like the distant future. Therefore, I will not present any long-term vision of our future, bearing in mind that there are too many external factors which can modify the prospects substantially.

In the short-term perspective, the beginning of real economic adjustment at the level of the firm is the most important development that is taking place. The effects of continuing privatization will become apparent in microeconomic performance, but they will bring with them certain social costs, such as increased unemployment and enhanced social mobility, to which the citizens have not been accustomed. Tax reform is another challenge both for the population and for the government. We shall have to handle the consequences of the break-up of the federation, try hard to maintain relations with Slovakia on the highest possible level and adjust our external relations to the new situation.

I believe in our deeper involvement in the process of

European integration. I am convinced that the next period will bring an inflow of billions of dollars of new foreign investments after the political situation in our country has become clear and stable. I do not expect any dramatic changes in economic policy, or new radical steps to be taken. We have already created the framework for the market economy to function and the future will concentrate more and more on strengthening our markets.

The main risk for the reforms is populism and lack of a clear and realistic political and economic programme. Right-wing dictatorship, however, is not a real danger in our part of the world.

Do you think your country can catch up, within a reasonable period of time, with the living standards of Western Europe? What, in your view, is a 'reasonable period of time'?

BALCEROWICZ: I think there is a good chance that these changes will be adopted, and Poland will be able to develop economically at a faster pace than on average in the west. Thus, the gap in the level of economic development between Poland and the west will gradually be closed. But this is certainly a long-term process. Such a prospect also requires access to western markets and stronger and stronger links with the European Union, rising to full membership in the not very distant future.

BOD: I would not forecast a development similar to the fast growth of the 'small tigers'. Hungary today is at a higher level of development than the Asian countries embarking on the rapid growth of the 1960s. At the same time, the dismantling of the old organizations and the release of the human and physical resources tied down in enterprises without prospects requires additional expenditure in the case of the Hungarian economy. The rehabilitation of the environment also implies costs. The inherited debt is an additional burden.

I expect an inflow of direct foreign investment, assuming access to external markets and the relatively fast social and regional diffusion of our internal capacity for modernization. I therefore forecast a modest growth from 1993, and, particularly after 1994, an annual of increase 4-5 per cent in GDP. Economically, this could raise Hungary to a level of advancement by the end of the decade that will make it primarily a political issue whether or not the European Union is willing to accept Hungary as a member.

KLAUS: I am convinced that our country will be back in developed Europe soon and all our efforts are aiming at this goal. We want to catch up with the level of economic development of Western Europe.

Finally, we should like to ask you what is the single most important piece of advice that you would give to your colleagues in Russia and the other former Soviet republics struggling to implement economic reforms similar to those that you were partner to in your country?

BALCEROWICZ: There is no way of avoiding risk; the only problem is to choose the right kind of risk. And the risk of delaying the difficult but necessary decisions is on the whole economically and thus socially greater than that of taking them immediately after assuming power.

BOD: What advice or recommendation can be deduced from the Hungarian experience for a country newly setting out on the road to democratization? Perhaps our discussions here show that significant differences can be observed even in the case of countries at a similar level of development and with similar historical backgrounds (Poland, the Czech Republic, Hungary). Nevertheless, if there is one piece of advice I could give – and perhaps I speak not as an economic policy maker but as a former researcher – I would underline the importance of *institution building*. The establishment of the legal, organizational and procedural institutions for the market is not enough, but, without them, a modern market economy cannot evolve. Building them certainly takes time. But, precisely because they are mainly based on universal principles, the setting up of national institutions can be speeded up by making use of international assistance.

KLAUS: To my Russian colleagues I would advise the creation of an organized political structure on a grass-roots basis capable of securing political support and stability for the implementation of the reform. The fate of the reform cannot be based on loose and random coalitions in parliament or on the deliberations and attitudes of a single charismatic leader.

Appendix: Data on the Design of the Reform Programme

Poland

Reform efforts in Poland prior to 1989 had concentrated on decentralizing decision making by increasing the autonomy of enterprises in terms of both setting prices and allocating inputs. So by 1989 Poland had substantially reduced the role of central allocation in the economy and only a number of prices were subject to limited controls. In 1989, however, the macroeconomic situation in Poland deteriorated rapidly. High inflation was locked in by full wage indexation. Budgetary expenditures soared and the deficit exploded. The financing of the deficit gave rise to a surge in the money supply and excess demand, putting in place the elements of hyperinflation.

The government that came into power in September 1989 opted for a strong stabilization package with the immediate liberalization of prices and trade. The 'shock' transformation strategy adopted in January 1990 entailed a sharp devaluation and unification of the exchange rate, the liberalization of prices and trade, a large reduction in subsidies (which helped curtail the fiscal deficit), a change in the tax system, a large increase in the cost of credit, and the imposition of controls on wage increases. Poland concluded a debt-reduction agreement with the Paris Club that reduced the current value of official debt by approximately 50 per cent.

140

While the private sector's share of the economy was relatively high, this was the result of the large proportion of the agricultural land that was in private hands. If agriculture was excluded, the state sector still accounted for over 90 per cent of production. The government envisaged the large-scale privatization of state-owned enterprises through a centralized approach. The unstable political situation in Poland has resulted in delay in implementation of the government's 'mass' privatization programme, which was approved by parliament only in mid-1993.

Hungary

Hungary began its process of economic reforms away from central planning in 1968, and by the second half of the 1980s important parts of the institutional and legal infrastructure for a market economy were in place. A modern tax system had been recently established that included personal income tax, value-added tax and an enterprise profit tax. On the financial front, a two-tier banking system had been set up to remove the role of credit allocation from the central bank. Unlike Czechoslovakia and Poland, Hungary had also gradually liberalized prices and trade over the preceding years, so a good portion of consumer prices and trade had been freed from government control prior to the collapse of the communist system. Thus, while Hungary did not depart totally from its economic past with the change of government in 1989, it did begin to significantly broaden the scope of economic reform and abandoned the commitment to market socialism.

At the beginning of 1990, Hungary faced a severe foreign exchange liquidity crisis and doubts emerged concerning the new government's commitment to continue the servicing of its foreign debt. To overcome this crisis, the government implemented a strict programme of stabilization that included exchange rate devaluation, a reduction in the budget deficit through expenditure cuts and tax increases, and a tight monetary policy. Prices and foreign trade were largely liberalized and all restrictions on private sector activity were eliminated.

In addition, the structural reform programme was accelerated. The government's programme featured the privatization of state-owned enterprises. The Hungarian authorities have not followed any single type of privatization ideology, but have implemented a series of policies that have evolved gradually. A distinguishing feature of the privatization process has been its reliance on a case-by-case approach rather than the adoption of a set of rules that applies to all cases.

Czechoslovakia

In many ways the initial structural conditions for the transformation to a market economy were less favourable in Czechoslovakia than in Hungary or Poland. The private sector was almost non-existent, economic activity was concentrated in large units, the legal and institutional basis for a market economy was largely absent, prices were still almost completely controlled, and a system of export and import taxes and subsidies isolated domestic producers from external competition. Furthermore, Czechoslovakia was largely dependent on socialist trade, with exports to and imports from socialist economies making up more than 60 per cent of trade. To its benefit, however, macroeconomic imbalances were not a serious problem. Inflation, both official and repressed, was low, the monetary overhang was relatively small, and hard currency debt was only 15 per cent of GDP. Fiscal and monetary policy had traditionally been conservative and the government budget had been close to balance for many years.

After the 'velvet' revolution of November of 1989, the new government began introducing reform measures. Retail subsidies on food were removed and the prices of gasoline, industrial energy and transport were increased. During the year there were two major currency devaluations, with the commercial and tourist exchange rates unified at the end of the year. The beginnings of a market-based financial system were established with the creation of a two-tier banking system. A good deal of time was spent preparing for the broad-scale launching of the transformation programme in January 1991.

The transformation programme consisted of price stabilization and structural reforms. Stabilization measures included a commitment to maintaining a balanced budget, and tight monetary policy with credit ceilings imposed on individual banks. An incomes policy was adopted to keep wage increases below the inflation rate by imposing a punitive tax on wage increases above an agreed level. The structural reforms included: (a) price and trade liberalization, (b) mass privatization of state-owned enterprises and (c) the development of a financial system.

Price liberalization was introduced in a 'big bang' fashion on 1 January 1991 with 85 per cent of turnover freed from price controls. Quantitative restrictions were retained only on oil and gasoline imports. An import surcharge of 20 per cent was imposed on consumer goods, falling by 10 per cent by January 1992. During the course of the year an additional 10 per cent of turnover was freed from price controls.

Privatization of state-owned enterprises was the central

feature of the transformation programme. The government's strategy consisted of (a) privatization of small enterprises through auctions and restitutions and (b) privatization of some 3,000 large enterprises through a combination of voucher sales to the public and direct sales to domestic or foreign investors. Roughly two-thirds of all voucher-holders entrusted their vouchers to privatization investment funds.

*Table 1. Initial conditions in Poland, 1989: Basic indicators
(percentages).*

Share of GDP :
    Manufacturing and construction   50.7
    Agriculture   12.2
    Services   37.1
of which
    Private sector   28.4

Share of employment:
    Manufacturing and construction   35.3
    Agriculture   28.5
    Services   36.2
of which
    Private sector   47.2

Direction of trade:

Share of exports
    Convertible currency   67.0
    Rouble   33.0
Share of imports
    Convertible currency   69.0
    Rouble   31.0

Openness (Exports + Imports / GDP)   34.0
External debt (per cent of GDP)   58.8

Price controls
    Share of free consumer prices   66.0

*Table 2.   Initial conditions in Hungary, 1989: Basic
              indicators (percentages).*

Share of GDP:

Manufacturing and construction	41.9
Agriculture	16.2
Services	41.9
of which	
Private sector	n.a.

Share of employment:

Manufacturing and construction	37.5
Agriculture	17.3
Services	45.2
of which	
Private sector	7.8

Direction of trade:

Share of exports	
Convertible currency	62.2
Rouble	37.8
Share of imports	
Convertible currency	61.6
Rouble	38.4
Openness (Exports + Imports / GDP)	63.3
External debt (per cent of GDP)	71.3
Price controls	
Share of free consumer prices	83.0

*Table 3.   Initial conditions in Czechoslovakia, 1989: Basic
indicators (percentages).*

GDP shares:

Manufacturing and construction	56.3
Agriculture	7.9
Services	35.8
of which	
Private sector	>5.0

Employment shares:

Manufacturing and construction	46.6
Agriculture	11.1
Services	42.5
of which	
Private sector	10.1

Direction of trade:

Share of exports	
Convertible currency	39.2
Rouble	60.8
Share of imports	
Convertible currency	37.7
Rouble	62.3
Openness (Exports + Imports / GDP)	67.0
External debt (per cent of GDP)	14.9
Price controls	
Share of free consumer prices	>5.0

Table 4.   Selected Economic Indicators for Poland.

	1988	1989	1990	1991	1992
(percentage change)					
Real GDP	4.1	2.0	-11.6	-7.0	0.5
Consumer prices[a]	73.9	639.5	249.0	60.4	44.3
Wages	83.9	283.0	365.1	59.8	25.2
Unemployment rate[b]	0	0.1	6.1	11.8	14
(in per cent of GDP)					
General government balance	0.0	-7.4	3.5	-6.2	-7.0
General government expenditures	48.0	48.8	44.7	49.0	51.0
(in billions of US dollars)					
Current account balance	-0.2	-4	0.8	-2.3	-3
External debt, net of reserves	37.1	39.1	44.4	47.3	50.0

Source: International Monetary Fund; World Bank; OECD; European Bank
        estimates.

Notes: [a] year end
         [b] end of period; per cent

Table 5. Selected Economic Indicators for Hungary.

	1988	1989	1990	1991	1992
	(percentage change)				
Real GDP	-0.1	-0.2	-4.0	-12.0	-4.6
Consumer prices[a]	14.8	18.9	33.4	32.2	21.6
Wages	24.8	18.6	22.9	28.5	25.7
Unemployment rate[b]	n.a.	0.3	2.5	8.0	12.3
	(in per cent of GDP)				
General government balance	0.0	-1.3	0.4	-4.6	-8.3
General government expenditures	61.4	60.2	56.9	61.4	60.0
	(in billions of US dollars)				
Current account balance	-0.8	-1.4	0.1	0.3	0.3
External debt, net of reserves	18.1	19.2	20.2	18.8	17.0

Source: International Monetary Fund; World Bank; OECD; European Bank
estimates.

Notes: [a] year end
[b] end of period; per cent

Table 6. Selected Economic Indicators for Czechoslovakia.

	1988	1989	1990	1991	1992
	(percentage change)				
Real GDP	2.5	1.4	-0.4	-15.9	-7.1
Consumer prices[a]	0.6	1.5	18.4	53.6	11.5
Wages	2.31	3.2	4.5	16.3	23.6
Unemployment rate[b]	n.a.	0.0	1.0	6.6	5.1
	(in per cent of GDP)				
General government balance	-1.5	-2.4	0.1	-2.0	-3.3
General government expenditures	59.5	64.5	60.1	54.2	52.8
	(in billions of US dollars)				
Current account balance	-0.1	-0.4	-1.1	0.4	0.2
External debt, net of reserves	6.2	6.8	7.7	8.3	8.6

Source: International Monetary Fund; World Bank; OECD; European Bank
       estimates.

Notes: [a] year end
         [b] end of period; per cent

Index